HEART OF HEAVEN MINISTRIES

PROMOTED FROM LEADER TO SERVANT

God's Heart for Those In Authority

by
Michael Adams

Published by
Heart of Heaven Ministries
www.heartofheavenministries.com
e-mail: info@heartofheavenministries.com

Cover design by inhousemarketing.net

First Edition

ISBN 13:   978-0-578-01378-7

<u>Dedication</u>

To my Father in heaven
for His grace, mercy, patience, and kindness;
and for showing me His heart.

To my wife, Debbie,
for being an incredible woman of God and
helping me share my life-message.

To my children, Jeff and Janna,
whom God has used since before you were
born to show me His heart.

And to my dad,
For teaching me The Lord's Prayer
when I was five years old.

<u>Acknowledgements</u>

I wish to thank the following friends and family
for helping make my first book a reality:

Debbie Adams
Janna Adams
Kandy Mill
Dr. Ed Roberts
Leslie Taylor
Bruce Wilkinson
...for your help with editing this book.

Michelle Adams at In-House Marketing
...for your help with the cover design.

My family, friends, and co-workers over the years
...for your invaluable part in the life experiences that have
helped shape whom I have become and enabled me
to share what God has given to me.

Table of Contents

<u>PREFACE</u>

This Book is My Testimony

I will not presume to speak of anything except what
Christ has accomplished through me, resulting in the
obedience of the Gentiles by word and deed.
Romans 15:18

Sometime during the summer of 2008, I listened as a pastor used the last half of Romans 15:18 to make a point in his sermon. His point was that our personal walk with God should reflect Him and His character in such a way that it inspires and encourages others to pursue Him themselves. His message was powerful and right on the money, but the first part of the verse lit up like a neon sign to my spirit and I did not hear most of the remainder of his sermon. The first half of the verse says, "I will not presume to speak of anything except what Christ has accomplished through me."

What so deeply impressed me about the first half of Romans 15:18 is that the Apostle Paul did not rely on the testimonies of other people to teach the Jews about the kingdom of God as he traveled from city to city; he spoke of his own personal encounters with the Father, Son, and Holy Spirit—his testimony. When I saw that truth, I was both greatly encouraged and greatly challenged. I was encouraged because I had already started writing this book. I was challenged because I realized that this book is really my testimony of my personal encounters with God. And my testimony, just like yours, is intended to inspire others to see value in pursuing a personal relationship with the Creator of the universe.

My primary gifting is that of service, as is spoken of in Romans 12:7. It is one of the gifts my Father in Heaven gave me, and it is the perspective from which I live life. So this book, "Promoted from Leader to Servant," contains what God has taught me about leadership during my entire life.

I remember the day He began that transition in my heart. I was working as a manufacturing planner of commercial jet aircraft. I was a self-starter, very good at what I did, and except for the occasional question I needed answered, I worked best when left to myself. As I sat at my desk pouring over a stack of technical drawings and formulating the strategy and sequence for assembling parts critical to the flight of an airplane, He said to my spirit, "You've worked by yourself long enough. Now I am going to teach you how to work with people." I knew in my heart what He meant. I was at the threshold of learning how to lead others and He had things to teach me about what that meant to Him.

I believe we are all eventually called to function in some form of leadership during our lifetime. That role may be as a father, mother, or caretaker within a family structure, or as a manager in whatever work or activity we choose to pursue. It really does not matter what form it takes; what matters most is how we approach the responsibility and what we understand our God-given role to be.

Man has one view of leadership. God has another. If you take one trip to the local library or bookstore, you will see that there already exists a wide variety of books written on leadership management styles and methods. At any one time, you will likely find over a hundred books on the subject written by a wide array of entrepreneurs, university professors, and successful leaders from the realms of business and ministry. I have read some of those books and acknowledge that they all contain good material, but many of them seem focused on teaching you how to get people to follow you. From man's perspective, that makes sense—the premise is that you are not a leader unless someone is following you! But in Matthew 20:26, Jesus said, "It is not so among you, but whoever wishes to become great among you shall be your servant." Jesus was not a leader because thousands followed Him. The fact is, thousands left Him when they found out what it meant to follow Him. He was a leader because He came to serve and to seek and save that which was lost (Matthew 18:11 and 20:28).

How can you be leader and a servant at the same time? Our western culture defines a servant as someone hired to work for another. But God has taught me that leadership in the kingdom of heaven is about serving to raise others up to become all that God has gifted them to be, not about getting people to follow me. That is what I understand the Word of God to say and that is the perspective of my testimony.

Why put my testimony in a book? Early one Saturday morning, I sensed the Spirit of God speak these words into my heart as I was taking a shower, "You could write your own book, you know." It took me by surprise, so I knew it was the Lord, and when He speaks like that, I've learned it is best to agree with Him. So, I silently responded, "Yes, I can," and what immediately followed for the next few hours was a detailed outline of the subjects and messages that were already deep within my heart and I sensed I was to include in this, my first book.

What I share in the following chapters is what God has taught me about being a leader. If you asked me to summarize what that is in just a few words, I would say it is "to *recognize, raise up,* and *release* people into their God-given gifts and destiny." That has become my passion and I pray that what I have to share—my testimony—will bless, inspire, and challenge you as you seek to become all God intends you to be.

INTRODUCTION

Promoted from Leader to Servant
God's Heart for Those in Authority

*See to it that no one comes short of the grace of God,
that no one be like a bitter root springing up and
causing trouble, and through him many become
defiled.*
Hebrews 12:15

In Hebrews 12:15, the Apostle Paul instructed the Christian Jews to make sure that no one came short of the grace of God. A complete reading of that verse says that falling short of the grace of God results in bitterness and the eventual defiling of others. What does it mean to "fall short of the grace of God?" It can mean many things, but within the context of this book, I believe we fall short of His grace either when we don't understand the gifts we've been given and what to do with them, or we don't use them fully.

That is why being promoted to a position of leadership is so important. This might surprise you, but **your promotion was not primarily for you!** It was so you could speak with His authority and help those He has placed in your care to fully realize the grace of God in them.

Paul's instruction includes a warning sign to leaders of every sort, especially Christian leaders. **The warning sign is this:** *behavior that is rooted in bitterness* (which causes trouble and defiles others) *indicates that a person has "come short of the grace of God."* To become an effective leader, at least from God's perspective, we need to understand the true message of this warning sign and know what to do about it. The "what to do about it" is contained in the following chapters.

Through much of the 20th century, the issue of church and organizational growth has been a hot topic, inspiring the writing of numerous "how to" books and classes at colleges and seminaries. At stake is their very survival, and many of those "how to" books propose methods and strategies designed to get people to follow a leader. The question many churches seem to struggle with is why their growth is primarily the result of believers moving between ministries, and their decline the result of good people moving on to something else. Why do they leave? Why do they not just follow? And why does there tend not to be an influx of pre-believers that just can't wait to "taste and see that the Lord is good" (Psalm 34:8)?

Businesses go through similar organizational growth and decline cycles, most commonly driven by the ebbs and flows of market fluctuations. But sometimes people move from organization to organization or company to company for more personal reasons; and it's not always about money.

To help today's leaders deal with the issues of planning and organizational growth, or the lack thereof, many consulting and research firms exist. Their services include personal coaching, strategic planning, business plan development, and seminars. They also provide a wide array of training materials, and pre-designed strategies guaranteed to result in growth.

For churches, the primary strategy for growth is to reach out to a segment of a local community using programs focused on building relationships with non-Christian men, women, and children in the hope they will then become disciples of Jesus Christ. To a degree, that is an effective strategy, but from my perspective, the main problem church leaders face is what to do with the people AFTER they have come in the door. Getting them into the building is relatively easy; keeping them there, however, is another story. It is the difference between giving people a reason to <u>visit</u> versus already having a solid reason for them to <u>stay</u>.

It is very similar for businesses. Even under ideal conditions, developing an efficient and effective workforce is difficult and expensive. It takes time for new employees to become accustomed to their new jobs and new relationships. They also come with a hope and expectation that they will contribute to the success of the organization. But something is wrong when an organization regularly loses 50% of its specialized new-hires to voluntary attrition by the end of their first year of employment. That happened in a company I worked in for almost 20 years. When we, the management team, asked why they were moving on, they simply said it was because they had become disappointed, disgruntled, and bored with the job we hired them to do. They felt their skills were being under-utilized and wanted work that was more challenging and interesting. In essence, they sensed they had "come short of the grace of God."

For many years, I have heard it said that in many organizations, and especially churches, about 20% of the people do

80% of the work. Assuming that statistic is accurate, have you ever wondered why that is true? I have come to believe it is rooted in the fact that most leaders are more focused on growing the size of their organization rather than helping every individual develop their gifts and then releasing them into their destinies.

My dad was one of those that dropped through the cracks of the church, and I know of many others that have either already walked away or are close to doing so. I believe he started out with a heart that was sensitive to spiritual things. In fact, when I was very young I remember him telling my mom that children should have some kind of spiritual training. Not knowing what else to do in this area, he regularly took our family to church and, as each of us turned about five years old, he would kneel with us by our beds and teach us to pray The Lord's Prayer. That foundation has never left me, but my father eventually turned his back on the church because it had become clear to him through a series of events that the church leaders were more interested in his money to maintain and build the church machine than they were in him as a person. Unfortunately, many men today feel the same way about the modern church.

While proof-reading the first draft of this book a friend commented, "Men are wired to fix, create, and make things work ,and sitting in the 'weekly Sunday lecture series' trains them to come to church prepared to disengage as they have learned that nothing is required or even desired of them. Many who have tried to contribute (their heart and gifts) have been shut down by the church leadership." Maybe that is why they choose to become married to their work and recreation. At work, they know they are wanted and valued for the gifts and skills that they possess. And when they come home, engaging in doing something fun and adventurous is more inviting than sitting silent and disengaged for two hours while a church leader passionately tells them from the pulpit that God loves and cares about them, and to not forget to tithe. To them, the person in the pulpit is representing God, and it is a stretch for them to believe God takes a personal interest in them when the person doing the preaching does not!

The truth is that God is more interested in growing people than organizations, and that goes for both businesses and churches. That is not to say there is anything wrong with organizations, they are necessary! But for the most part, man's focus is on growing the "machine" while God's focus is on growing the people. Does God have a plan for growing people? I believe He does.

People with strong natural leadership skills tend to see people as assets, things to be used, controlled, and taught to serve those in charge. In contrast, the kingdom of heaven says people are **gifts FROM the Lord**, possessing **gifts OF the Lord**, and given **assignments BY the Lord** to work together and accomplish **amazing feats FOR the Lord**—feats that span every area of life, not just church.

So this book is about a different leadership model. It is not about teaching you how to get others to follow you. In fact, if you are a naturally gifted leader you already know how to do that. It is about teaching you, as a leader, how to help those under your care become all God intends them to be—so they do not fall "short of the grace of God."

This book is also about helping Christian leaders create what I call a "Spirit-led" atmosphere—an environment in which the Holy Spirit is free to move and reveal the directions and strategies of God through EVERY individual. It is about helping *"visionaries"* and *"implementers"* (two new terms we will define later) learn how to honor and value each other's strengths and weaknesses so they can effectively work together. It's also about seeing not only the practical and spiritual gifts God has put inside each person (including yourself), but realizing that each person is actually God's gift to the world, thus making room for Him wherever His gifts reside (Proverbs 18:16).

At this point, you might be asking what a "Spirit-led" atmosphere looks like, and what you could expect to see happen in such an atmosphere through those under your care. Those are great questions! I will give you a personal example that I am privileged to share with you.

In 1985, I got my first real taste of receiving a Spirit-led strategy from the Lord that I will never forget. At the time, I was working as a Tool and Production Planner for The Boeing Company. In an effort to find new ways to reduce costs, the company encouraged every employee to submit suggestions for just about anything, including changes to business and manufacturing processes, aircraft design, and the like. Being a dedicated team player, I walked out into the final assembly area of the factory one afternoon and quietly asked God to "give me an idea." At the time, my area of expertise and responsibility was the propulsion sections of the 707, 727, 737 and 757 aircraft, which included anything and everything to do with the structure and systems for the main engines and the auxiliary power unit installed on the airplanes.

Immediately after making my request, a very specific part re-design came to mind along with the words *eccentric bearing*. When I discussed the idea with my senior lead later that afternoon, he thought I was crazy and said it would never work. But I believed the Lord had given me that idea and proceeded to work closely with the engine strut design engineer to develop a viable solution. The result was amazing! That one part redesign saved the company more than $100,000 in annual production costs by eliminating over 70 hours of delayed work on every 737 and 757 airplane we built. In addition, I received a $10,000 suggestion award, the most available at that time. However, my greatest reward for that suggestion came sixteen years later, when I discovered the redesign was not only still in use, but its use had been expanded to other airplane models and had never caused a production problem! That absolutely made my day!!! From my perspective, that was truly a Spirit-led strategy that God used to bless me, my family, and the company; and it never failed to work!! (Yeah God!)

Something similar to that can happen to you and your organization, but it is important to note that Spirit-led strategies are not something we do; they are something we receive. And there is only one way we can receive them—by making a place for the Holy Spirit to move freely in our midst, which really means in our hearts, and then being obedient to do whatever He says to do. In other words, we need to create an atmosphere in and around us that is **inviting to the Holy Spirit.**

It is my experience that the Holy Spirit does not openly reveal Himself in the midst of strife and confusion. He reveals Himself where there is love, joy, peace, patience, kindness, goodness, faithfulness, gentleness and self-control (Galatians 5:22). So creating that positive atmosphere is what invites Him to move freely. And as we endeavor to do that, I believe God wants everyone He has placed in a position of authority to understand and embrace three key points, which are the foundations of this book.

1. First, **God speaks to and through every one of His children to reveal His strategies.** No one is exempt from receiving from Him.

2. Second, from the perspective of the kingdom of God, **true leadership serves first** by **recognizing the gifts** God has already placed **in ourselves** and **in those around us** to help us collectively accomplish what He has put in our hearts to do.

3. Third, **true leadership in the kingdom of God** is about **raising others up** into what God has called them to be and to accomplish; with the intent to **release** rather than hold on to or control. For a leader, it is about helping your subordinates rise up and succeed, not about making you look good to your superior. For a parent, it is about launching your children into their destinies. For a spouse, it is about helping your chosen mate become all God intends them to be as a husband, wife, father, or mother.

In the following chapters, I will present fifteen subjects from a different scriptural perspective than what you are probably accustomed to hearing. I say "different" because I have never heard any other preachers, teachers, or business people share some of what I will share with you. And from what God has taught me about leadership, I believe these fifteen subjects are important for every

Christian in any position of authority to consider as they seek to create an atmosphere that is conducive to receiving Spirit-led strategies for their organizations from the people in their care.

One final but very important note before we move on—I have purposely avoided any use of the word *leader* throughout the remainder of this book, except in a few instances where no other word would suffice. I did so because in Matthew 23:10 Jesus told the people not to seek to be called leaders (teachers or guides) because He (Jesus) is our One and only Leader. Then in verse 11, He goes on to say, "The greatest among you shall be your *servant*." Therefore, in keeping with Jesus' instructions, I use the term *servant(s) in (or with) authority* in the place of *leader(s)*; a terminology change that I believe is both biblically correct and long overdue in our modern day world.

You might be wondering why Jesus made such a stinging point about seeking to be a servant rather than a leader. I believe He had two reasons.

First, as mentioned above, Jesus is the only person to whom God ever gave the position and title of *Leader*, and Jesus has not given that position away to anyone. He has only extended to us *authority to act in His name* (Luke 9:1).

Second, the heart of man is easily enticed and intoxicated with the power that comes with authority, which frequently leads to abuse, favoritism, elitism, nepotism, and selfish ambition. God's intention in granting authority to individuals has never been so they can lord it over others; that is the way of the kingdom of this world (of man). In God's kingdom, He gives people positions of authority for one primary purpose and privilege—to serve others and raise them up. New Testament leadership is not about being the top dog of loyal followers; it is about being their greatest champion—serving, equipping, and helping them to become all that God intends them to be. That was and continues to be Jesus' model; the model for us to follow.

You might also find it interesting to know that a review of the use of the words *leader*, *servant*, and *serve* in the New American Standard Bible yields a fascinating statistic, at least for those interested in the statistics of word usage and their importance in understanding God's priorities. What I found was that the word LEADER occurs just 151 times, while the words SERVANT and SERVE occur collectively 1,093 times. Clearly, God has chosen to call those He has given authority to as *servants*, not *leaders*.

I pray that you will be both challenged and inspired by what the Lord has given to me to share with you.

CHAPTER 1

Peter the Fisherman—
Tender or Shepherd of Sheep?

Simon Peter said to them, "I am going fishing." They
said to him, "We will also come with you." They went
out and got into the boat; and that night they caught
nothing.
John 21:3

I have often felt like Peter and the other disciples in John
21; following the Lord for so long and then feeling like I'm
all alone and wondering where He went! When I have
been in that state, going back to "fishing" has looked very attractive,
at least on the surface. And He knows I've tried to go that direction a
number of times! But He never seems to let me do that, at least not
for long.

In John 21, Jesus had already been crucified and resurrected
and had appeared several times to the disciples, but He had not yet
ascended to heaven. The entire city was probably still in quite a stir,
and being one of His followers was not popular. I am not sure exactly
what was running through their minds, but from the account in

scripture, it would appear that Peter and the other disciples were at their height of despair and deeply missed their daily interactions with Jesus. In fact, I would not be surprised if they sat or walked around town wondering what to do next. Regardless, they finally decided to do what most of us do when we feel discouraged, lost, and unsure of what lies ahead—we go back to doing what is familiar because it gives us a sense of stability. For them, they returned to doing what they knew best—fishing.

So Peter and the others spend the night out in their boats but catch absolutely nothing. Then early in the morning, as they are cleaning their nets and possibly talking about how uneventful and unprofitable their efforts were, someone calls to them from the beach and tells them to try again, but to toss their nets into the water from the other side of the boat. After hauling in more fish in one catch than they had ever done before, John tells Peter, "It is the Lord!" Peter then jumps ship and makes his way to shore, where they all gather and have a sunrise breakfast with Jesus. Wow! That must have been quite the cure for the devastating events that had just occurred! Then Peter has an intriguing discussion with Jesus that, I believe, reveals something of what God is looking for in the heart of everyone that aspires to be in any kind of leadership role. Let's look closely at John 21:15-17 and 19.

> So when they had finished breakfast, Jesus said to Simon Peter, "Simon, son of John, do you love (*agapao*) me more than these?" He said to Him, "Yes, Lord; you know I love (*phileo*) you." He said to him, "Tend my lambs" (v15).
>
> He said to him a second time, "Simon, son of John, do you love (*agapao*) me?" He said to

Him, "Yes, Lord; you know I love *(phileo)* you."
He said to him, "Shepherd my sheep" (v16).

He said to him a third time, "Simon, son of John, do you love *(phileo)* me?" Peter was grieved because He said to him the third time, "Do you love *(phileo)* me?" And he said to Him, "Lord, You know all things; You know that I love *(phileo)* You." Jesus said to him, "Tend my sheep" (v17).

After he said this, Jesus told Peter in verse 19, "Follow me."

According to Vine's Expository Greek Dictionary, *agapao* is used to express the "deep and constant love and interest of a perfect Being towards entirely unworthy objects, producing and fostering a reverential love in them towards the Giver, and a practical love towards those who are partakers of the same, and a desire to help others seek the Giver." Some boil this kind of love down to being *unconditional*. Vine's goes on to say, "In Jesus' first two questions, *agapao* suggests a love that values and esteems. It is an unselfish love, <u>ready to serve</u>."

In contrast, again as described in Vine's, "The use of *phileo* in Peter's answers and the Lord's third question conveys the thought of cherishing the Object (not the love and interest of a perfect Being) above all else, of manifesting an affection characterized by constancy, from the motive of the highest veneration (profound respect and reverence)." Some describe this kind of love as being *conditional*.

The main contrast between the two words is in their focus. *Agapao* is focused on the true interests of people—ready to value, esteem, and serve them. *Phileo*, on the other hand, views people more as objects—cherishing and appreciating them, but not really willing to sacrifice self for their well-being.

What is most interesting, however, is the progression and regression of what Jesus asks Peter to do in response to Peter's answers.

In verse 15, Jesus asks Peter, "Do you *agapao* (love, esteem, and are ready to serve) me?" Peter replies, "Yes, I *phileo* (cherish and appreciate you)." Then Jesus says, "Tend my sheep." (Notice that it would have been more accurate for Peter to have responded, "No, I don't *agapao* you, I *phileo* you.")

In verse 16 Jesus asks Peter a second time, "Do you *agapao* (love, esteem, and are ready to serve) me?" Peter responds again with, "Yes, I *phileo* (cherish and appreciate you)." Jesus says, "Shepherd my sheep."

Then just for good measure, Jesus asks almost the same question a third time, but in a way that enables Peter to answer with what is actually in his heart. In verse 17 Jesus asks Peter, "Do you *phileo* (cherish and appreciate) me?"

At this point Peter, probably somewhat frustrated and grieved because He knew Jesus caught the fact that he could not say, "I *agapao* you," says, "Lord, You know all things; You know that I *phileo* (cherish and appreciate you)." Then Jesus says, "Tend my sheep."

Typically, the key words expounded upon in this scripture passage are *agapao* and *phileo*, but while those words are important, I want you to see two other key words—*tend* and *shepherd*—both of which imply significantly different levels of heart commitment to those under a person's care.

According to the American Heritage Dictionary, *tend* means to have care of; to watch over or look after; to manage the activities and transactions of; to attend to or serve, to apply one's attention to. Therefore, someone who *tends* is essentially a hireling, one who does well at "tending the store" when they are there, but has no personal ownership or long-term interest in the overall well-being of those over whom and what he is attending to. Loyal employees, regardless of their level of how much they are paid, are often great *tenders*, but because they have no significant emotional or financial investment in the business or ministry in which they serve, they are free to move on whenever they please. They are not true *shepherds*.

The duties and responsibilities of a *shepherd*, however, are much more encompassing and imply a much greater degree of interest, involvement, and commitment. A true *shepherd* not only *tends* to the needs of his sheep, he also guides, teaches, and shows them the way, acting as a mentor, pilot, chaperone, and protector. In ancient times, the *shepherd* was the only thing that stood between a flock and the animals that preyed upon them. A *shepherd* that was incapable of fending off the attack of predators may well have lost his or her own life. Since a *tender* would have likely gone home when the sun went down, the *shepherd* needed to be ready to lay down his life for his flock because most predator attacks came under the cover of night.

Based on John 21:15-17, I believe Jesus was asking Peter, "Are you ready to be a *shepherd,* and to serve others as I have served you?" Unfortunately, Peter knew in his heart that he was only ready to be a *tender*.

Where are you today? Do you *agapao* Jesus? Are you ready to become a *shepherd* of those you are now to serve? Or, are you already a real *shepherd*—ready to lay down your own life for the life of your *sheep*?

Maybe you are only prepared to *phileo* your flock—to *tend* to their needs as best you can while watching out for #1. Don't feel bad if you must answer as Peter did. Jesus understands. It is for that reason He said in verse 19, "Follow me." But what does that really mean? Where is He going, and how do we follow Him?

In the next chapter, we will look at where Jesus is going and what drives the heart of the Father, the Son, and the Holy Spirit—we will look at God's vision, mission, and strategic plan.

CHAPTER 2

God's Vision, Mission, and Tier 1 Strategic Plan

For God so loved the world that He gave His only
begotten Son, that whoever believes in Him should not
perish, but have eternal life.
John 3:16

In your role as a *servant in authority*, you will eventually need to develop some kind of a plan for leading those under your care. That plan may include increasing the effectiveness and influence of the company or organization that you oversee. It will likely be referred to as a "strategic plan" and include *vision* and *mission* statements, as well as some level of detail that describes the steps you will take to accomplish your goals. Or as a leader in your home, it will likely outline how you intend to function as a husband and father, or wife and mother.

Have you ever realized that God has a *vision*? His *vision* is simple and eternal, and whatever *vision* you have, God wants your *vision* to connect with His.

He also has a *mission statement* and *strategic plan*. You might not think about it in those terms, but since vision and mission statements and strategic planning have become "the thing to do" in both businesses and churches over the past 20 years or so, I think it's valuable to realize that those concepts are not new. They existed before the beginning of time!

If you were to see it written on heaven's wall or displayed on a fancy poster near His desk, I imagine God's *vision statement* might read something like this:

> *That everyone I create has the opportunity to live*
> *their entire life, both on earth and after their earthly*
> *life, in close fellowship with Me.*

Who is *everyone*? Jeremiah 1:5 says, "Before I formed you in the womb I knew you..."

I believe *everyone* means every person that has existed before us, exists now, and ever will exist. It includes those who choose to receive God's gift of salvation through Jesus Christ and those who do not; those living anywhere in the world, doing anything. Why does He include everyone? First, because He created our spirits and *knew* each one of us before we were conceived, and second, because He gave us as His gifts to the world around us (more on that in another chapter). We are all God's created children.

Does that include the people that outrightly reject Him up to the moment they die? Are they also His children? Yes, they are! In Luke 15:11-32, the father of the prodigal son never once considered his wayward child not to be his son! He never lost his place in the family, but that son used his power of choice to choose where he lived his life. That is why in Luke 15:24, Jesus refers to the son as "dead" and "lost." But as soon as the son "came home," his father was overjoyed with his return and embraced him as the son that he always was.

The significance of that story is as much about our origination as it is about our final destination when our physical life on this earth ends. We are eternal beings and we will spend the after-earth portion of our lives either with God in heaven or without Him in hell. Those who reject God during their earthly life will not spend their life in eternity with Him in heaven, but rather with the family they chose to align themselves with—Satan and the rest of the angels that followed him (Revelation 21:5-8). That is the essence of the story of the prodigal son in Luke 15.

So God's *vision*, that everyone He creates has the opportunity to live their entire life in close fellowship with Him, was (and still is) so important to Him that He made it His *mission* to provide a way for His *vision* to be accomplished. To accomplish His *vision*, He provided His Son as payment for our sins and then gave us only one responsibility—to choose between His Son and Satan. And the evidence of our choice would be in what we believe in our heart and say with our mouth. All we need to do is *believe* in His provision *and speak* out our profession of that belief (Acts 16:31 and Romans 10:9).

Since God has a *vision* and *mission* He wants to accomplish, you may be wondering if He also has a *strategic plan*. I believe He does, and that it consists of three phases. It is documented throughout the Bible, but if He were to put His plan in a one-page format, His single page Tier-1 strategic plan might look something like what's on the next page.

THE KINGDOM OF HEAVEN
My Eternal Vision, Mission, and Strategic Plan
Author: God

My Vision:	That everyone I create has the opportunity to live their entire life, both on earth and after their earthly life, in close fellowship with Me.
My Mission:	To provide everyone every possible chance to experience My love for them while on earth, and a way for them to spend eternity with Me.
My Plan:	**Phase I:** 1. Send Jesus to earth to live and die as they do, but without sinning. 2. After He pays the penalty for their sins, resurrect Him from the dead and have Him be at My right hand for the rest of eternity. STATUS: Complete
	Phase II: 1. Identify the people on earth that are faithful to Me. 2. Inspire them to recognize the different gifts I have given each one and work together to represent Me to everyone around them. 3. Give some of them positions of *servants in authority* over others and assign them the responsibility to teach them how to know Me, hear Me, obey Me, and love Me. 4. Have those serving in positions of authority teach the rest of My children how to follow Me so when they graduate from their earthly lives to their eternal lives they will have already trained their replacements. STATUS: In progress and on-going until everyone has been given the opportunity to choose Me, and all whom I know will choose Me have done so.
	Phase III: 1. At the end of the age that I have established for life to exist on earth, separate My children in every generation who chose to follow Me from those who chose to reject my constant invitations and efforts to love them. 2. Bring those children who chose to follow Me into the heavenly places I have already prepared for them. 3. Send those children who chose not to follow Me into the place I have already prepared for the devil and the angels that rebelled against Me. STATUS: The start of Phase III depends on how My children progress through Phase II. I will not activate Phase III until Phase II is completed and I am the only one that will know that day or hour.

My point is that God's *vision* is both eternal and primarily for our benefit, not for His. How and where we end up is the only *vision* that has eternal significance to Him.

One more thing I want you to notice is that Phase II of God's strategic plan can only be effectively accomplished by *"whoever believes in Him"* (John 3:16). In other words, unless you, as a *servant in authority*, absolutely believe in Him only for salvation, you will lead people away from Him, not to Him. Therefore, to be effective in your role as a *servant in authority*, you will need to develop a plan for leading those under your care and a strategy to ensure your trustworthiness to them. To earn their trust, you will need to speak with the voice and the heart of our Father in heaven because He has given you authority to act in His name.

To illustrate what I mean, consider John 10:27. Jesus said, "My sheep hear my voice, and I know them, and they follow Me; and I give eternal life to them, and they shall never perish; and no one shall snatch them out of my hand."

Early one morning many years ago when our two children were very small, my wife and I were going through a very trying time. I cannot remember the specific issue we were dealing with, but I will never forget the encounter I had with God as I stood at the kitchen sink cutting up an apple to take in my lunch that day.

The Lord said, "My sheep hear My voice. Your wife and children are My sheep. If they are not listening to you it is because you are not speaking My voice."

A flood of tears came to my eyes. It was not my intention to hurt them, but His rebuke was loud and clear. When I do not reflect the heart and voice of my heavenly Father, His sheep whom He has placed under my care will not listen to me.

God has designed His sheep to follow His voice, the voice of the *Good Shepherd*, and resist the voice of a *tender*. So it is with every *servant in authority*. The best feedback you can pay attention to is how those under your care listen and relate to you, and whether or not they trust you. If you claim to be a man or woman of God and yet have constant friction with those under your care, the problem is most likely with you more so than it is with them. And until you come to a place of getting your own view of the situation in line with God's view by the pursuit of hearing and reflecting the voice of God on a daily basis, it is unlikely that things will improve.

So how can we become trustworthy *shepherds*, able to hear and speak God's voice? It begins with what we seek, because what we seek is indicative of what resides deep within our hearts. And our choices are simple—we either seek His kingdom or we don't.

In the next chapter, we will look at what it means to seek His kingdom and we will discover the three foundation stones that are crucial to becoming an equipped *servant in authority*.

CHAPTER 3

Where Do We Start?

Seek first His kingdom and His righteousness,
and all these things will be added to you.
Matthew 6:33

6:33 A.M.

I am continuously amazed and challenged with this number. In fact, there is hardly a morning that goes by that I do not see 6:33 as I glance at the digital clock radio that is conveniently positioned near my pillow or at the clock on the microwave or stove in the kitchen. The strange thing is that I never sit and stare at the clock until it reaches 6:33, it's just there as I am either waking up, getting dressed, or getting something in the kitchen. The other fascinating part is that it typically only happens in the morning, rarely in the evening, and it's been happening for several years.

I am convinced that it is not a coincidence that I glance at the clock and it shows 6:33. To me, it is a reminder of Matthew 6:33, which says, "Seek first the kingdom of God and all these things shall be added unto you."

When I began recognizing the frequency of seeing 6:33, I started asking God to clarify what He was trying to tell me. Was I to do more activities and work harder for Him? Was I to volunteer more time at church? Did He want me to sit on a park bench or in a local coffee shop and evangelize those who walked by? The list of possibilities went on and on, but the point is that I always wondered if seeking His kingdom meant being more active in some way. Fortunately, I have come to see that He was not trying to tell me that at all!

One Sunday morning, as I sat waiting for church to start, I opened the bulletin of announcements and read something that put Matthew 6:33 into perspective for me. Oddly enough, it was not a pastoral sermonette or some encouraging word by a great saint that caught my attention. It was the words on a flyer announcing a women's weekend retreat. It said, "The kingdom of God is righteousness, peace, and joy in the Holy Spirit." The full quote is in Romans 14:17-18, which says, "For the kingdom of God does not consist of food and drink, but righteousness, peace, and joy in the Holy Spirit. For the one who serves Christ in this way is pleasing to God and approved by people."

I sat absolutely amazed and relieved at the simplicity of His message. Seeking His kingdom first did not mean building a huge ministry, getting others to follow me, doing more volunteer work, feeding thousands of homeless people, or praying great prayers of faith that healed people of horrible diseases or emotional bondages. Seeking His kingdom simply meant seeking *righteousness, peace, and joy in the Holy Spirit as my #1 priority while I work, play, and interact with people on a daily basis.* These three character qualities are the foundation stones of an equipped *servant in authority.*

But how do I **seek righteousness**? How do I **seek peace**? And how do I **seek joy in the Holy Spirit**? I have never considered myself an expert on any of these areas, but I can share with you what God has been teaching me about them.

SEEKING RIGHTEOUSNESS

To seek righteousness means to pursue being *in right standing with God.*

What does *right standing* mean? Let's look at three points to answer that question.

First, *right standing* **simply means to stand in right relationship with God.** According to the American Heritage Dictionary, the definition of the word *right* is "conforming to justice, law, or morality; in accordance with fact, reason, or truth." So standing in right relationship with God means that I not only believe IN God, but that I also actually BELIEVE God. There is no way I can stand *right* before Him without doing both of those things because He is the only One in the universe that is *right* all of the time!

Psalm 119:160 says, "The sum of Thy word is truth, and every one of Thy righteous ordinances is everlasting." From God's perspective, His word is eternal and is the foundation He has given to show us what is *right* in His eyes—which is where we often fall. I don't know about you, but in my more than 32 years of walking with the Lord, it has been far easier for me to believe IN God than it has been to BELIEVE God by believing and trusting what He says. I am not proud to say that; I am just stating a fact. But the truth is that we are unable to stand rightly before Him without both believing IN Him and BELIEVING Him. God challenged me with that truth during one of my "quiet times" one morning. He said, "Believing Me is believing every word I say. Are you willing to do that?" As soon as He said it, I realized that meant <u>every</u> word.

Fortunately, the life-long process of learning and growing IN God includes opportunities for us to practice BELIEVING God—a process that, by design, is part of our earthly journey. I am happy to testify that I am much farther along in actually being able to believe God in the challenges I face than I was even just a few years ago!

Second, being in *right standing* with God means aligning my values that I live by every day with what God says is valuable to Him.

This too is not easy because we all face the daily challenges of having to live IN this world but not be OF it; enjoying the beauty and creativity of His creation (including His children) without allowing the sinful desires of our flesh to rule our choices. So the question is, how do we establish a value system that enables us to be in *right standing* with Him? There is only one answer—**we must choose His value system.** We must call "good" what He calls good, and "bad" what he calls bad. If we don't, we will be out-of-sync with Him.

Isaiah 5:20-21 describes God's heart on this point:

> Woe to those who call evil good, and good evil; who substitute darkness for light and light for darkness; who substitute bitter for sweet, and sweet for bitter. Woe to those who are wise in their own eyes and clever in their own sight.

Third, *right standing* **means letting Him live IN me so that He can live THROUGH me** in all I think, do, and say. That means having no unconfessed sin in my life.

1 John 1:6-9 says the following:

> If we say we have fellowship with Him and yet walk in the darkness (sin) we lie and do not practice the truth; but if we walk in the light (His truth), we have fellowship with one another, and the blood of Jesus His Son cleanses us from all sin. If we say we have no sin, we are deceiving ourselves, and the truth is not in us. If we confess our sins, He is faithful and righteous to forgive us our sins and to cleanse us from all unrighteousness.

This passage says we cannot choose to live in sin and expect to stand *right* with God. We can only have fellowship with Him if we walk in His truth. And if we try to apply our personal version of "truth" to Him, we are deceiving ourselves—He won't buy the lie!

Right standing requires spending time with Him daily and asking, "What do You want to say to me today?" It means seeking to be in 100% agreement with what He says about me and the world around me, and accepting His loving discipline when He shows me an area where my attitudes and beliefs do not line up with His.

So *seeking righteousness* is the first foundation stone of being an equipped *servant in authority*. Let's go to foundation stone number two—*seeking peace*.

SEEKING PEACE

Seeking peace **means pursuing a relationship with God that allows His peace to reside WITHIN us, so that we become carriers of His peace to those AROUND us.** When we live from that place of God's peace being within, we will naturally establish and maintain an atmosphere in and around us that is not hostile or unsafe toward others.

How do we seek and implement His peace in and around us?

When we first learned about spiritual warfare many years ago, we were encouraged to shout at the devil, binding and commanding him to be silent and get out of our way. Being the relatively non-confrontational person that I am, that seemed like an appropriate tactic to learn in order to deal with demonic interference. However, my view has changed in the past few years.

Currently, we attend a church that has a very different view of waging spiritual warfare, and the approach we have learned has yielded much greater fruit than I would have ever imagined. Their approach is to pray and *release the peace of God* over an area rather than to command the demons to leave "in the name of Jesus." What is fascinating about this approach is that it has a profoundly positive effect on the people and atmosphere of the area. Romans 2:4 says, "...the *kindness* of God leads people to repentance," and in Matthew 10, Jesus instructed the disciples to give a *blessing of peace* when they went into a new household. As we have learned to release God's *peace* over individuals and regions, we have seen His *kindness* settle and cause many to encounter the true and living God. As a result, people feel drawn to the *kindness* of God through us, rather than feeling "confronted" about their sin by us.

I have had the opportunity to pray for people from around the world that visit or call our church wanting prayer and, at times, counsel for their current crises. I frequently pray that God's peace, grace, mercy, and kindness would settle on them, their family, and their situation. At the end of our time, they often testify that they sense a spiritual blanket of peace resting upon them, which enables them to hear and receive the answer God has for them.

There are many other benefits to seeking the peace of God and having His peace reside in us, but of the 353 verses in the Bible that talk about peace, I would like to mention just a few that describe a positive impact on ourselves and our families.

- His *peace* in us sets the stage for the success of our future generations (Psalm 37:37).

- His *peace* is indicative of wisdom (Proverbs 3:17), becomes as a guard to our hearts and minds (Philippians 4:7), and keeps us from stumbling (Psalm 119:165).

- His *peace* is a fruit (or result) of the presence of His Spirit in our lives (Galatians 5:22).

SEEKING JOY IN THE HOLY SPIRIT

In one sense, *seeking joy in the Holy Spirit* is simple to me—it is **being thankful and glad to have the Holy Spirit in my life, helping me to hear and understand the voice of God** in the midst of every-day living. But the concept of being joyful in the midst of very difficult circumstances always challenged my understanding. Fortunately, in the past few years God has helped me see His bigger picture, and getting a glimpse of His perspective has enabled me to begin to have genuine "joy in the Holy Spirit."

I believe it is best described in James 1:2-4, which says, **"Consider it all *joy*, my brethren, when you encounter various *trials*,** knowing that **the testing of your faith produces *endurance*.** And **let** endurance have its perfect result, so that you may be perfect and complete, lacking in nothing."

Notice that God ties the concepts of **joy**, **trials**, and **endurance** all together. In fact, James implies that we will never be "perfect, complete, and lacking in nothing" without successfully being *joyful* as we walk through trials that build endurance.

We all want the full blessings of God (to be perfect, complete, and lacking nothing), but James says that we will not receive those blessings without first developing endurance. And endurance can only be obtained one way—through trials that test our faith. Now get this—**when we** *seek joy in the Holy Spirit* (Romans 14:17-18) **we are**, in fact, **giving God permission to give us whatever tests and trials are necessary to produce a faith of endurance within us.** It is in the midst of those trials that we are to *enjoy* the presence of the Holy Spirit as He helps us work through the circumstances. Think of it as a process that makes us more durable—capable of withstanding spiritual wear and tear or decay.

Let me give you a practical example from the manufacturing world—the process of heat-treating metal and other materials. A metallurgist will use the processes of heating and cooling to make a material either harder to make it stronger and more resistant to damage, or softer so it can be used more easily.

Many years ago I had the opportunity to watch the heat-treating process at work. The company I worked for made wear resistant parts for road building equipment. After forming, the soft steel parts went to the foundry and were heated to a very high temperature and then cooled rapidly. Depending on how long the entire process lasted, the parts were either hard all the way through, or just partially hardened. When done correctly, the hardened parts were able to endure a very long time in the machines used to make roads of asphalt and concrete.

That is what God's trials are meant to do for us—give us the ability to endure difficult circumstances and environments. But to successfully pass His test, we must genuinely appreciate the presence of the Holy Spirit helping us pass the test. That is *having joy in the Holy Spirit.*

It is easy to *have joy in the Holy Spirit* when things are going well and we have no trials. But when we *seek joy in the Holy Spirit*, we must realize that that level of joy only comes encased inside the shell of trials. In the big picture, God is making us more durable so that we can withstand ever increasing amounts of spiritual "wear and tear;" refining and polishing us to reflect His image to those around us; and preparing our hearts to enjoy eternity as we rule and reign with Him.

In summary, as we *seek first the kingdom of God*, the foundation stones of His *righteousness, peace*, and *joy in the Holy Spirit* become like solid rocks, firmly planted under our feet. And as we stand on those solid rocks, we stand in a spiritual atmosphere that invites the Holy Spirit, enabling Him to give us His strategies that will both equip and enable us to accomplish the assignments He has given us to do.

Do you have the foundation stones of *righteousness, peace, and joy in the Holy Spirit* under your feet? If not, ask God to help you seek them. He wants to give them to you. In fact, He's just waiting for you to ask and be willing to weather the trials that it will take to produce endurance within you.

When you have those foundation stones under your feet, you are ready then to receive the *vision* and *strategy* for implementation that God wants to give you.

Now, take note of what time it is when you awaken tomorrow morning. God may be speaking to you through the clock in your bedroom!

CHAPTER 4

Visionaries and Implementers

Where there is no vision (revelation), the people are
unrestrained, but happy is he who keeps the law.
Proverbs 29:18

Record the vision and inscribe it on tablets that
the one who reads it may run.
Habakkuk 2:2

When I left Boeing in 1998, my deepest prayer was, "Open the eyes of my heart." In fact, the song by that name written by Paul Baloche brought me to my knees every time I heard it, which at that time, was almost daily. As I sat praying at my desk in my home office in mid-2000, I asked God again to "open the eyes of my heart" and show me what He had gifted and called me to do. Here was His response:

I have called you to come alongside "visionaries" and "implementers" to help them put together the plans and processes they need to accomplish their vision.

I was a bit surprised at His response because I had run away from doing exactly that about a year earlier! Since then, I have been on a journey in which God has brought greater clarity of what He meant by the terms *visionaries* and *implementers* and what it means to *come alongside*. But before I give you the details of what the Lord showed me I need to define those words for you. They are not "black" and "white" terms, but rather a description of gifting versus acquired ability within individuals.

So, what are *visionaries* and *implementers*?

Visionaries are incredible people; and I have a great respect for what God has gifted them to do! Here are the three primary positive traits of a *visionary* the Lord showed me:

1. They are "big picture" people with a gift to *see* the impossible—what <u>could</u> be accomplished.

2. They have a zeal that *inspires others* to join them.

3. They frequently have fresh new ideas to share.

Implementers are also incredible people; and I have a deep respect for what God has gifted them to do as well! They too have three primary positive traits.

1. *Implementers* thrive on feeling useful and being able to help *visionaries* accomplish "big picture" goals.

2. They are extremely detail-oriented and are natural experts at seeing all that needs to happen to make the "big picture" a reality.

3. They receive great satisfaction from achieving clear objectives and have the tenacity to "stick with it" until every little detail is accomplished.

Those are the strengths of the *visionaries* and *implementers*, but I have heard it said that our greatest strengths are also our greatest weaknesses, which I believe is true. When taken to an extreme, our strengths can actually hinder our ability to work with one another. So I would like to look for a moment at the weaknesses of both as well. We will look first at the *visionaries*.

By temperament and gifting, *visionaries* tend to be *high control* personalities and do not easily *let others run* without their hands-on guidance; sometimes even resorting to *micro-managing*. This isn't necessarily a bad thing, but it can be, especially if they micro-manage because they have trouble trusting the heart and abilities of the implementers around them.

In addition, because of their "big picture" perspective, *visionaries* are not typically skilled at leading the effort to develop the detailed plans, budgets, and processes they will need to fulfill their own vision and do not really enjoy participating in such things. They may be able to talk for hours about their ideas and what they would like to accomplish, but their attention span when working out the details is very limited. (It has been my personal experience that two hours of detailed planning can be like an eternity to the *visionary!*) The daily routines of planning and implementing feel restrictive, like drudgery, and often interfere with the time they need to dream and process the new ideas and visions they frequently receive. Unfortunately, these weaknesses can greatly hinder the ability of the implementers to "run" with the vision.

Visionaries also tend to have so many ideas on a daily basis that they frequently change direction mid-stream before much of anything regarding their vision gets accomplished. This can be very unsettling for the implementers because frequent direction changes typically result in very little work actually getting accomplished — and accomplishing tasks is what every implementer thrives on!

Now let's look at the weaknesses of the *implementers*.

Because of their attention to detail, *implementers* can become stuck in the details of the plans and processes they use and miss the opportunity to adjust when the "big picture" changes or needs to change. This can be equally frustrating to visionaries because the vision may be constantly evolving and the team needs to evolve with the vision. The visionary may feel bound to an immovable rock when an *implementer* is stuck in the details and unable to adjust when the "big picture" changes.

In addition, by temperament and gifting, *implementers* are very cautious people, weighing the pros and cons of every choice and decision because they do not want to make a mistake or because they want to avoid the inevitable "rework" that comes when decisions are made without adequate understanding. While this strength can help the visionary avoid pitfalls and "stay the course," it becomes a weakness when God is telling the team to step out and "trust Me." When God asks us to trust Him He is saying that He will not tell us all of the details and we must let go of the familiar, at least to some degree, to move forward. Doing this can be very difficult for the *implementer* because *implementers* love stability, and trusting the unknown is, by definition, unstable.

So, what is the typical outcome of the relationship between *visionaries* and *implementers*? How do their respective strengths and weaknesses affect one another?

Unfortunately, when both *visionaries* and *implementers* become frustrated and discouraged with each other, they become ineffective as a team. When that happens, the *visionaries* may then look for a new team, and the *implementers* may eventually become unwilling to commit their time, effort, and personal resources to fulfill a vision and plan that either is unclear or is constantly changing. The results are evident in many places and look something like this:

1. 20% of the people do 80% of the work.

2. Many gifted *implementers* leave the business, ministry, or project and avoid helping because they do not see how their *gifts* fit into fulfilling the vision.

3. The *visionary* rarely accomplishes the vision.

That is not the heart of God for either *visionaries* or *implementers*! God gave us the gifts we have and it is His intention that we honor and cherish each other for what we each bring to the table. But how do we do that? How can we work together to establish a positive atmosphere for receiving Spirit-led vision and strategies? What is the solution?

The solution is simple to state but difficult to accomplish because it requires *trust,* and real trust is very hard to come by these days. Two verses from Proverbs and Habakkuk describe the intended relationship between *visionaries* and *implementers.* And from those two verses there are three activities that must happen for any team of *visionaries* and *implementers* to effectively work together. Here are the verses:

Proverbs 29:18

Where there is no vision (*revelation* in the Hebrew language), the people are unrestrained.

Habakkuk 2:2

Record the vision and inscribe it on tablets that the one who reads it may run.

The three activities implied by these two verses are:

1. Get a vision

2. Write it down

3. Let others run to accomplish the vision

Let us first look at Proverbs 29:18.

People are "unrestrained" when they lack vision (or revelation) from God because vision provides focus; focus requires boundaries; and boundaries require a structure (law) within which to work. Without those three elements—**vision, focus, and boundaries**—people are ineffective relative to their potential. Boundaries and structure create an environment within which people can effectively function to accomplish the vision, and people are happiest when they have a sense of genuine accomplishment within a well-defined structure. That is why the role of the *visionary* is so important. Without a vision to follow, people do not have much chance of fulfilling their full potential.

Now let's look at Habakkuk 2:2.

Writing the *vision* on *tablets* (something everyone can see) helps everyone stay focused on the goal, respecting the boundaries, and working within the structure.

If you do not believe that, consider the converse. When people gather and no one has a vision to accomplish or do something, the group flounders and someone eventually asks, "Well what do you want to do?" "I don't know! What do you want to do?" And so forth. At some point, either someone suggests something to do that everyone jumps on, or they part ways until another day. What is the difference? The difference is *vision*. *Vision* inspires the group to stay together.

But in order for *implementers* to *run* with a *vision*, the *vision* needs to be *written down* (made clear) and then *released* to them. That is where trust comes in. It is very hard for *visionaries* to trust *implementers* with their vision, especially if others with *selfish ambition* have stolen or destroyed their visions in the past. (We will talk more about *selfish ambition* in a later chapter.) To the *visionary*, a vision can be like a child, and entrusting a child to someone else is not a natural thing for any parent to do.

God designed *implementers* to serve and accomplish every vision they resonate with; and *implementers* are like skilled nannies, able to help *visionaries* raise up "their child" by creating and implementing the plans to make the vision a reality. But they cannot truly *run* unless *visionaries* are able to trust *how* they run—able to release the *gifts* that lie within them.

So *visionaries* need to trust, and *implementers* need to be trustworthy. I hope that this helps you understand why the foundation stones of *righteousness, peace,* and *joy in the Holy Spirit* we talked about in Chapter 3 are so important to becoming an equipped *servant in authority.* Without them, we have a difficult time both trusting and being trustworthy.

How can *visionaries* and *implementers* learn to live and work together? The solution lies in the following chapters.

CHAPTER 5

God's Gifts to All His Children

He gave gifts to men.
Ephesians 4:8

I want to share with you a revelation the Lord showed me near the conclusion of a biblical counseling class I attended a few months after I left Boeing in 1998. What He showed me totally rocked my view of *spiritual gifts* and excited me because it was truly one of those revelatory moments that made me feel like a huge light bulb had just "lit up" inside my spirit.

The counseling class lasted twelve weeks. During the last few weeks of class, a very seasoned woman of God was teaching us about *spiritual gifts*. She used three New Testament passages to present her teaching. Much of what she shared was review for me; but toward the end of the week, I believe I received a "rhema" word from God about the role the God-head has in giving gifts to His children. I realized that the New Testament talks about unique gifts we receive from the *Father*, the *Holy Spirit*, and the *Son—and in that order*. I had never seen spiritual gifts that way before; and as she was teaching, the Lord showed me three key revelations:

Revelation #1

Out of His mercy and grace, it is the Father that gives each person natural abilities (gifts) so they can be fruitful and multiply during their life on earth.

Romans 12:1,3-8 says:

> I urge you, brethren, **by the mercies of God**, to present your bodies a living and holy sacrifice, acceptable to God, which is your spiritual service of worship...**God has allotted to each** a measure of faith. For just as we have many members in one body and all the members do not have the same function, so we, who are many, are one body in Christ, and individually members one of another.

> Since we have **gifts that differ according to the grace given to us**, each of us is to exercise them accordingly; if prophecy, according to the proportion of his faith; if service, in his serving; or he who teaches, in his teaching; or he who exhorts, in his exhortation; he who gives, with liberality; he who leads, with diligence; he who shows mercy, with cheerfulness.

Though I understand the Greek word for God in this passage is Theos, which can be translated as the Trinity, I saw this passage in a different light that day. I saw that before we are physically born, the

Father, through His grace and mercy, gives us abilities (gifts) to enable us to provide for our families, and to succeed at living with and for one another. We typically consider these "natural" abilities because they are evident within us from a very early age. These *gifts* include *prophecy, service, teaching, exhortation, giving, leading (serving in a position of authority), and mercy,* and they don't change when someone becomes "saved." I believe that is why we see these same gifts and qualities active in people who have not yet come to know God; because their Father in heaven (the God-head, or Trinity), whom they have yet to meet, gave them those gifts out of His grace. Let me give you an example.

Several years ago, I had the privilege of being the production manager of a full-length feature film. While taking a lunch break from shooting one day, the production crew and actors were all sitting around a picnic table at a city park. This park was right next to a low-income housing project that housed veterans and others who were on some form of public assistance. While we munched on our catered sandwiches, an elderly street person stopped by our table and asked, "Do you have any extra food that you could spare to give to me?"

I am sorry to admit, inside of me a little skirmish began as I weighed the potential ramifications that might result if we gave him some food. This area was a haven for beggars and if we fed one street person, others would likely approach us. Knowing we did not have the budget or the time to do that, I was wrestling inside about what to do. So while I was trying to discern, "What would Jesus do?" the director of photography, who was not a Christian, immediately said, "Sure! I don't need all of this food. You can have half of my sandwich." As soon as he said that I felt both grieved and ashamed, sensing that I had just missed a significant God-opportunity.

When I got home that night, I continued to feel disturbed about what had happened. So when I woke up the next morning, I asked God to show me why the entire incident still bothered me. As I confessed my sins of selfishness and fear, He let me see the reason why the photographer so willingly gave up half of his sandwich. It was because one of the *gifts* he had received from the *Father* (or God-head) was that of *giving,* just as is mentioned in Romans 12:6-8.

At the end of my time with God that morning, I asked Him what I should do. I sensed Him say to me, "Confess your own sin to him, and then acknowledge My gift of giving that I placed in him. Tell him that it blesses Me when he uses that gift." So when I got to our first shooting location that morning, I did just what God asked me to do. My acknowledgment touched us both deeply and established an even greater sense of trust and respect between the two of us than I could have imagined. I believe it also validated the Father's love FOR him by verbally recognizing the gift of giving the Father GAVE him.

Revelation #2
The Holy Spirit gives us supernatural gifts so we can communicate with the Father, Son, and Holy Spirit.

I Corinthians 12:4-11 says:

> Now there are varieties of gifts, but the same **Spirit**. And there are varieties of ministries, and the same Lord. There are varieties of effects, but the same God who works all things in all persons. But to each one is given the

manifestation of the **Spirit** for the common good. For to one is given the word of wisdom through the **Spirit**, and to another the word of knowledge according to the same **Spirit**; to another faith by the same **Spirit**, and to another gifts of healing by the one **Spirit**, and to another the effecting of miracles, and to another prophecy, and to another the distinguishing of spirits, to another various kinds of tongues, and to another the interpretation of tongues. But one and the same **Spirit** works all these things, distributing to each one individually just as He wills.

Next, God showed me that when we become Christians by confessing our sins and declaring Jesus as our Lord and Savior, the Holy Spirit gives each of us "supernatural" gifts to meet specific needs in God's kingdom. These *gifts* enable us to *tune in* to God so He can speak to us and work through us to accomplish greater things than we can accomplish with the natural abilities we received at conception. These *gifts* include words of knowledge, words of wisdom, tongues, interpretation of tongues, prophecy, distinguishing of spirits, faith, healings, and miracles.

Some might say the *gifts* given by the Spirit overlap with the *gifts* given by the Father in that both list *prophecy*. Is there an overlap? I don't think so.

I believe the difference may be that the *gift of prophecy* from the Father, being spiritual in nature, is active whether we are saved or unsaved because we have a human spirit that connects itself to the spiritual world around us. The difference, then, lies in the level of heaven we are tapping into—the second heaven (which is dominated by Satan and the other fallen angels) or the third heaven (in which the Father and Son reside and the Holy Spirit receives His instructions to impart to us). The *gift of prophecy* from the Holy Spirit taps into the third-heaven realm.

<u>*Revelation #3*</u>
The Son gave the Church gifts in the form of apostles, prophets, evangelists, pastors, and teachers (trainers) to equip others and ensure the growth of His Kingdom for many generations until the end of time.

Ephesians 4:7, 8, 11-13 says:

> To each one of us grace was given according to the measure of **Christ's gift...He gave gifts to men** (v7-8).

> And **He (Jesus) gave some as apostles**, and some as **prophets**, and some as **evangelists**, and some as **pastors** and **teachers**, for the **equipping of the saints** for the work of service, to the **building up of the body of Christ**; until we all attain to the unity of the faith, and of the knowledge of the Son of God, to a mature man, to the measure of the stature which belongs to the fullness of Christ (v11-13).

Notice that the gifts given by Jesus are not character qualities. Apostle, prophet, evangelist, pastor, and teacher—these are assignments given to equip others to do the work of the ministry in whatever realm they are called to serve. Some say these are offices of leadership. That may be so, but I do not believe they are offices we are supposed to seek to occupy, like president or manager. My personal opinion is that **they are promotions given by Jesus to those who have been faithful servants of the Lord.** Here is my rationale:

I see the *gifts* of the Father, the Holy Spirit, and the Son as progressive. That is what so excited me when God breathed that revelation into my heart. They are progressive in that:

First, God the Father gives everyone enough basic *gifts* that they have "the power to make wealth so that He may confirm His covenant which He swore to your fathers (Deuteronomy 8:18)." Even though He knows who will and who will not follow Him, He gives everyone every chance possible to succeed in this life. He has NOT withheld any *gifts* you or I need to live and prosper on this earth!

Second, as soon as people commit their lives to Him as believers, He gives them His Holy Spirit. The Holy Spirit allows them to have an open communication line with Him 24/7 for the rest of their lives, and they can accomplish supernatural things that they could not otherwise accomplish with just the *gifts* they received from the Father at conception.

Third, just as our physical growth is a progression, so too is our spiritual growth. As we live life, learning first to use the *gifts* we receive from the Father, then the *gifts* we receive from the Holy Spirit, the Son rewards us as *faithful believers* with a promotion. What is the promotion we receive from the Son? It is a promotion to serve out the rest of our days on this earth as apostles, prophets, evangelists, pastors, or teachers—**to equip the next generation so they are prepared to do the same** when we, the seasoned warriors, pass on from this life into the next.

What saddens me, however, is that our *gifts* are not always welcomed everywhere we go. In one place, our *gifts* can be recognized and received like a tall glass of fresh ice water in the midst of a desert where everyone is dying of thirst; and in another, they can be easily ignored or considered to be of little or no value to those around us. Have you ever wondered why that is? I have.

The reasons can be many and varied, and I am not discounting the fact that sometimes we might actually be carrying emotional baggage that sends "reject me" signals. But sometimes that is not the case. Sometimes the problem is not with us. Sometimes it is because *visionaries* and *implementers* are unable to recognize the value and significance of the *gifts* God has placed on their doorsteps in the form of people—His children.

In the next chapter, we will talk specifically about children—God's gifts to the world.

CHAPTER 6

"Children"
God's Gifts to Accomplish His Vision

Children are a gift of the LORD.
Psalm 127:3

"Before you get to your driveway we need to talk
about what happened back there."

That is what God said one night as I was driving home from a private meeting with one of the pastors of the church we attended some years ago. I remember it was about 8:45 p.m., dark and raining. We lived out in the country, about six miles from the church; and I was only about a mile from our driveway. I remember winding through the curves of the two-lane road, watching closely for anyone coming around a corner on the wrong side of the double yellow line. While I was paying attention to the road, I tried to understand what had just happened. As I mulled over the recent discussion, I was not expecting God to say anything to me, but He quite obviously had something significant on His mind that He wanted to teach me, hence, His interruption. "Okay. What do you mean?" I responded within my heart. But before I go on it would be helpful for you to understand some details about my meeting.

About a month earlier, I had submitted a written proposal to the church outlining a ministry plan my wife and I wanted to volunteer to do at the church. My request made the rounds up through the senior pastor and finally to the pastor in charge of the church's prayer ministry. My meeting was with this particular pastor to talk about our proposal. We were requesting permission to use one of the church's rooms once a week to host a video training class on inner healing prayer ministry. My wife and I had attended the training a couple of years before and had gone through significant counseling ourselves before being approved to host their classes, which we wanted to begin doing so as soon as possible.

During our one-hour meeting, I sensed the pastor and I were not on the same page; and yet I could not understand where he was coming from. He seemed resistant to my request but was not giving me any insight as to why. At one point, he asked me straight up, "Why do you want to host these classes here?"

I responded, "We have benefitted tremendously from the healing and training we've received, and we want to make the gift we have received available to others."

He said, "So, you think you're God's gift to the world!?"

His question caught me off guard, and my reflex response was, "No. I am not saying that I am God's gift to the world. I'm just saying we want to make available to others the gift of inner healing that we received."

Our meeting ended shortly thereafter when I was bluntly informed that I would never be given the opportunity to host the classes at the church. I thanked him for his time, got into my truck, and began the six-mile drive home. Now, back to my conversation with the Lord...

"My Word says that 'children are a gift from the Lord.' From My perspective, when do you stop being a child?" God asked. I knew this had to be a trick question! As I pondered where He was going, my spirit responded, "Never?"

"Exactly. You **never** stop being a child in My eyes. You said you were not My gift to the world. You were not telling the truth. You ARE My gift to the world. In fact, everyone I create is My gift to the world, and I've put inside each of you My gifts so that you might help one another. When church leaders understand that all those eyes looking at them on Sunday morning are actually the gifts I've provided to help them accomplish what I've asked them to do, they will then succeed at the level I have intended."

I was both stunned and humbled. Not in a bad way, but more like the way you feel when He just shows you a part of His perspective that is very different from your own; and you realize there is really no valid response other than to agree. I felt corrected, but I also felt a great peace. He had shown me something about myself and the people around me that I had never seen before.

By this time, I had turned off the main road, driven down our long gravel driveway, and parked by our garage. As I sat in the dark, I could hear the soft sound of the rain hitting the roof of my truck. In retrospect, maybe the rain was indicative of God's tears as He weeps over His children and the misunderstanding many of them face as they seek to use the gifts God has given them to help others. At the time, I was walking through that grief myself and as I sat quietly in my truck I realized, "I AM God's gift to the world, and I am NEVER to believe or say otherwise. Not only me, but EVERYONE is God's gift to the world. They are His gifts to me, and I am His gift to them. What He has put in me is to benefit them, and what He has put in them is to benefit me."

As I sat pondering His message and trying to decide when to go into the house, I realized that position, education, and level of responsibility have nothing to do with the gifts that we are. No one is higher, and no one is lower. We are just all different, and He has made us to be so—to be *gifts* to those around us.

A WORD FOR THE *VISIONARIES*

Implementers are God's gift to you. God placed within them the skills, perspective, patience, and perseverance to identify and attend to all the details it takes to accomplish the vision God has given you. They are His "runners," and runners love to race and win. **Let them run. They** *need* **to run.** In fact, one of your most important jobs is to clear the track so they can run without falling or having to contend with obstacles, including those rooted in your insecurities of how they may run.

Do not be afraid of what they can do. Trust what God has put within them. He has given them the capacity to tap into His heart to receive Spirit-led strategies and convert your vision into a Spirit-led plan. Will they make mistakes? Sure! Will they sometimes be afraid of the unknown? Absolutely!! Will they try to harness you, like a wild mustang in a corral, or make you feel like you are dragging a heavy weight? Yes!!! But God has given them the *gift of caution* and designed them to hear and see the strategies from Him that you need. Give them guidance, but let them *run*. Let them *exercise* their gift-muscles. Do not "muzzle the ox while he is threshing" (Deuteronomy 25:4 and 1 Timothy 5:18).

As you let them run, be careful to avoid overloading the *implementers* He has given you. Be sure that the vision you impart to them is truly the *revelation* that He has given you and your team to accomplish. Once you are sure, commit your time, effort, and resources to making that vision become a reality. Your implementation team needs you to focus and be committed to both the vision *and* to the implementation of the vision.

Take note that your greatest strength (being a *visionary*) is also your greatest weakness; and if left unchecked, you will tend to flood your implementation team with the hundreds of great ideas (visions) that are running around in your head at any given moment. The problem is that many of those visions will not all be true *revelations* from God, and your God-given gift of motivating *implementers* will result in you overwhelming them because the zeal you exude will give them the impression that everything you speak needs to happen or be started right away.

Take adequate time to know which *visions* are truly *revelations* of the Lord and write them down (Habakkuk 2:2). Then ask the Lord for the "when" of the vision so your implementation team can run with the "now" visions without feeling like your ideas are ping pong balls being randomly shot all over the room.

Lastly, realize that *God will use your implementation team to stretch and sharpen you* (Proverbs 27:17). How will He do that? He will use them to help you develop the disciplines you need to become a better *servant in authority*. A real life illustration will best explain what I mean.

While living out in the countryside for five years after returning from serving in YWAM in Hawaii, I was introduced to a very committed Christian *visionary* who believed God had given him a *revelation* that he would be the "owner of many businesses." He had owned a successful business years earlier until a serious accident took him out of commission, resulting in he and his wife losing everything. A mutual friend introduced us and the *implementer* gift within me seemed to fit well with his *visionary* gift. While we created a plan to realize his vision, God brought into his life a number of other very gifted *implementers* that agreed to serve as directors and advisors to what eventually turned into a real corporation. Our *visionary* was the CEO (chief executive officer) and I served as COO (chief operations officer). We then added a president and a few key advisors.

Before we actually incorporated, we had an opportunity to buy a fledging business that the *visionary* had once worked for—the first of many acquisitions, we believed. One of our advisors was a former executive vice president of a major international corporation. He was a Christian; wise, seasoned, and highly respected, having walked closely with the Lord for many decades and experienced in managing mega-million dollar projects. He was also a personal friend of our CEO and *visionary* leader. During one of our director meetings, we were discussing the opportunity we had to buy the fledging business. This wise and seasoned advisor gave us what I believed was incredibly sound advice. He said, "Plan to buy and successfully build one business first. As you prove you are able to succeed with one, investors will gladly help you buy more."

Shortly after delivering his advice, our advisor left the meeting. We continued our discussion, and everyone on the board (including the investor that was considering funding the purchase) agreed with the seasoned advisor—except one. The only dissenting voice was our *visionary* CEO, who said, "I will not limit myself to buying only one business at a time. God said I would have many businesses!" Our meeting ended shortly thereafter with no clear direction agreed upon, and our investor deciding to take more time to make his decision. The investor/board member eventually decided to place his money elsewhere.

Several months later, the team met again—this time in the living room of our home in the country. Following a great time of prayer, I presented a strategic plan that I had put together for us to review and discuss that afternoon. Included in the plan was a list of action items that each of us needed to accomplish so we could move forward. We also talked about the need to have weekly or bi-weekly review meetings to status our progress and to identify any new action items we needed to address. Everything seemed to be going fine until our CEO (the *visionary*) began to emphatically declare that no one was going to give him a list of things to do, establish a timetable, or in any way restrict his freedom to do whatever he wanted on whatever timetable he chose. In about one minute's time, he had informed the entire management team that he would not allow himself to be held accountable to any strategic plan or schedule of action items, even if they were for the good of the company.

I do not remember if I responded to his outburst, but I do remember sensing in my spirit that we had reached a dead end; and that I had just witnessed the beginning-of-the-end of our efforts to work together. The meeting ended shortly thereafter, and I spent the next few days collecting my thoughts. When the dust settled, I realized that after investing over a year and a half of my time to help him achieve his vision, he could not receive and embrace the management gifts his implementation team and advisors possessed. I stayed on for a little while longer, hoping things would change; but when another similar issue arose a month or two later, it was clear that I needed to resign my position. I did so the day after we became an official corporation.

Within a year, the company folded. All the *implementers* left his side and went on to other things. The last I heard, the *visionary* was working on reviving his vision and assembling a new team around him. It saddened me because it did not need to turn out that way.

A WORD FOR THE *IMPLEMENTERS*

Visionaries are also God's children, and He has given them as a gift to you. Why? Because you need them just as much as they need you!

Proverbs 29:18 says, "Without vision (revelation) people are unrestrained." Your *gift* for getting implementation revelations (i.e. Spirit-led strategies) from His Spirit is best used and made whole in the context of fulfilling a *revelation* that God has imparted to His *visionaries*. But just like you, *visionaries* are not perfect. Their zeal and seemingly endless *revelations* will at times frustrate you because they may not be able to tell the difference between what is truly a *revelation* and a great idea. Or they may lump a bunch of revelations together that God does not intend for you to implement all at the same time, or even in the near future! As co-laborers, you need to learn to work together and to take each idea before the Lord and ask, "When?" and "If now, how?"

You will also have to maintain an acute awareness of what is really in your own heart. *Implementers* have the *gift* of caution and yet tend to fear the unknown. And like the *visionary*, our greatest strength is also our greatest weakness if left unchecked. A missionary friend of ours recently helped me see this more clearly.

We were discussing how to know when to step out and trust God in a certain situation. I personally needed and deeply wanted his counsel on this subject. During our conversation, he said to me, "You are an engineer. By gifting, engineers are cautious; and they have to be! Without the gift of caution things like airplanes, and automobiles, and everything else under the sun that man has invented would not be safe to use." Wow, did I feel affirmed! No one had ever said that to me before!! Then he continued, "But God doesn't always want you to live there. There are times when you will not know all the answers, and you are not supposed to. It's in those times that He wants you to have faith in Him."

His final statement brought a sense of both peace and balance back to my heart. *Caution* IS a *gift* in an *implementer*; and as long as it is not overtaken by fear it is a benefit, not a liability, to the *visionary* and the implementation team.

A WORD TO BOTH *VISIONARIES* AND *IMPLEMENTERS*

One last point I would like to make applies to both *visionaries* and *implementers*. It is the fact that regardless of what we are, we are much like millstones and we need to be careful how we use our strengths and weaknesses. Let me explain.

Since ancient times, grain has been ground into flour using millstones. Millstones come in pairs—one designed to be stationary and the other movable. To be effective, they must be very heavy and contain both cutting edges and grooves. The cutting edges grind the grain into flour and the grooves channel the flour out from under the grinding surfaces. To operate properly, the millstones need to be balanced and positioned with a precise amount of separation between each other to ensure they produce the best flour. When used as designed, they are an incredible asset to a miller, producing flour that feeds many. When used any other way, however, the millstones produce nothing of value relative to their intended purpose.

As I mentioned earlier in this chapter, we are all God's children and we never stop being so. In Matthew 18, Jesus talks about our position as children in the kingdom of heaven. He says that **when we receive each other we are receiving Him.** Conversely, **when we reject any of His children, we are rejecting Him.** The passage I am talking about is Matthew 18:1-6:

> At that time, the disciples came to Jesus and said, "Who then is greatest in the kingdom of heaven?" And He called a child to Himself and set him before them, and said, "Truly I say to you, unless you are converted and become like children, you will not enter the kingdom of heaven. Whoever then humbles himself as this child, he is the greatest in the kingdom of heaven. And **whoever receives one such child in My name receives Me;** but **whoever causes one of these little ones who believe in Me to stumble, it would be better for him to have a**

> **heavy millstone hung around his neck, and to**
> **be drowned in the depth of the sea."**

No matter our age, we are always His children. And we are like millstones. When we receive one another and embrace the *gift* God has made each of us to be, including ourselves, then we will be able to work effectively together to transform His "grain" (vision) into usable "flour" (vision realized) capable of "feeding" the people of this world that are spiritually starving. But if we let our strengths become weaknesses, we can "drown" others, and even ourselves.

As I close this chapter, I would like to give you an example from my own life that illustrates the sad effects of the lack of personal vision, misunderstanding the gifts God gave me, and not embracing the *gift* He made me to be. I share this with you as a "how-not-to" story.

When I left my job at Boeing in September of 1998, we sold our home in Washington and moved to Kona, Hawaii, to work at the University of the Nations, a branch of Youth With A Mission (YWAM). In early April 1999, a friend of mine who was in charge of another YWAM ministry was helping the University overseers develop a long-term plan for expanding their facilities to support the growing number of students who were coming in from around the world. Early one afternoon, I received a call from my friend inviting me to a meeting at 2 o'clock at the administration building. He gave no explanation or any insight into the meeting's agenda; but the urgency in his voice indicated that I needed to be there.

I arrived shortly before 2 o'clock. The conference room was about half filled with the top and senior-most *servants in authority* of the university. When I inquired about the agenda for the meeting, they told me that they had just completed a major revision to their vision and mission statements and now needed help developing a strategic plan to implement their newly refined direction. As they further described where they wanted to go, I asked each of them to define more clearly the outcomes they wanted to achieve. As they answered, I wrote the thoughts that were coming to me on a large white board hung on the wall at the opposite end of the room. After filling up much of the white board with notes, I turned around and was surprised to see about half of the men in the room with tears in their eyes. The look on each of their faces indicated they were truly humbled and overwhelmed. Quite surprised (and a little afraid), I asked, "What's wrong?" (When people are crying there's obviously something wrong! Right?) They said, "Nothing. We've been in missions most of our lives, some of us for over 30 years, and we've never thought like this before."

Over the next few months, I used an entire wall of that conference room to document the plan we developed; and they used that plan to teach new staff, students, visitors, and potential donors where the University was headed. They were ecstatic!

Unfortunately, despite the way God had moved during the YWAM meetings, I did not fully understand what He had put inside me and how to be a partner with Him in all things. I had recently come from a corporate environment where "rational thinking" prevailed and into a world where "hearing and obeying the voice of God" was the primary requirement for success. As I worked with the university team, I understood the practical value of what I shared with them; but I was not confident in my gifts or the gift God made me to be, and I was having a very difficult time discerning whether what I was hearing was from the Lord, or just my own mind.

As a result, I ran. We sold our recently purchased condominium and moved back to the mainland and onto five acres in the country. Once there, God insulated me from the rest of the world for five years while He gave me a very different opportunity—learning how to get closer to Him. The results have been life changing.

CHAPTER 7

Your Gift Creates Room for You...Somewhere

A man's gift makes room for him
and brings him before great men.
Proverbs 18:16

He who receives you receives Me,
and he who receives Me receives Him who sent Me.
Matthew 10:40

In this chapter, I would like to look at the verses above from a very different perspective than is traditional. In the last chapter, I shared a dialogue I had with the Lord one night on the way home from a meeting with a pastor. That night, the Lord made it very clear that *we* are *His gifts* to those around us and to the world at large. But we are not only *His gifts*, we **carry** *gifts* in the form of **abilities**, **talents**, and **motivations** designed to make room for us. That is the subject of this chapter—your *gift* makes room for you.

Have you ever considered how your *gift* makes room for you?

Proverbs 18:16 says, "A man's *gift* makes room for him and brings him before great men." This was the case when the Queen of Sheba visited King Solomon to witness first-hand his fame and fortune she had heard so much about from others in her day. 1 Kings 10:2 says, "She came to Jerusalem with…camels carrying spices and very much gold and precious stones." King Solomon received her into his kingdom and granted her desire by showing her the treasures of His (God's) house.

An unselfish gift given with a pure heart expresses honor, gratitude, and appreciation for the recipient. That *gift* **prompts the recipient** to *make room* for the giver out of thankfulness and reciprocity because the recipient feels highly esteemed.

In Matthew 10:40, Jesus says, "He who receives *you* receives *Me*, and he who receives *Me* receives *Him who sent Me*." In other words, when we receive each other and the *gifts* we bring, we also receive God, the creator of the *gifts* within us. When people receive **us** as His *gifts*, they are actually receiving **Him**. As *servants in authority*, we must recognize that in order to get Spirit-led visions and strategies, we must be able to recognize and receive God in those He brings our way.

I believe it is God's heart for all *servants in authority* to proactively embrace the *gifts* (people) that He sends their way and make room for the *gifts* (abilities, talents, and motivations) they carry with them. In doing so, they are welcoming the kingdom of God in their midst!

Matthew 10 illustrates what I mean. In verse 1, *Jesus gave* His twelve disciples **authority** over unclean spirits. In verses 5-7, **He sent them out** and told them to declare, "The kingdom of heaven is at hand." Knowing some would accept and others would reject them and their message, He further instructed them in verses 14 and 15 saying, *"Whoever does not receive you,* nor heed your words, as you go out of that house or that city, *shake off the dust of your feet.* Truly I say to you, it will be more tolerable for the land of Sodom and Gomorrah in the Day of Judgment, than for that city." Finally, in verse 40 He says, *"He who receives you receives Me, and he who receives Me receives Him who sent Me."*

That sounds pretty harsh! Why did Jesus say that? I believe He said it for this reason:

He was sending them *HIS gifts*
(His disciples; His messengers),
to bring them *HIS gift*
(the kingdom of heaven).

In other words, He sends His people to bring His kingdom. He deems both highly valuable; and both are there to make room for Him! **When we reject *His* messengers (gifts) and the *gifts* they carry, we are saying, *"I don't have room for You, God."***

I believe God wants His *servants in authority* to realize that many of the people coming to them have arrived because God has led them to their doorstep. Therefore, it is very likely that they possess *gifts* needed by the organization or group they have come to join.

Consider this scene for a moment. You are interviewing a potential new employee, or having a brief visit with a guest or member of your church. Do you, as a *servant in authority*, recognize the *gift-set* they possess? Or do you only see them as a "white elephant" gift—to be discarded or given away to another as quickly as possible? If you do see them as a gift from God, are you looking for ways to equip and release them in their gifts? Your response during and long after your meeting will make it obvious whether or not you recognize and appreciate the *gift* God has placed before you.

Now, I realize that you may have multiple applicants for one job and you cannot be expected to hire every applicant. I understand that some people are just in the process of seeking to find their place. Yet it is important to realize that there is *some place* for everyone to serve, and it is our responsibility to recognize that truth and respond appropriately. Let me illustrate what I mean.

Shortly before being promoted to the position of Lead Tool & Production Planner at Boeing, I was given an assignment to recreate the manufacturing and tooling plans required to build the engine nacelles (support structures) for the first model of the 737 aircraft. Boeing had a long-standing policy that they would supply spare parts for any Boeing aircraft still in service, and at least one of the first seven aircraft built was still in service at that time. Unfortunately, someone had scrapped the plans and tools for those parts by mistake. My assignment included selecting and leading two employees to do the work.

I was informed that I could choose anyone I wanted from the 30 or so employees that worked within our wing structures group. My selections were to be submitted to my senior lead and supervisor the next morning, so that evening I went home and began asking God for direction. The names of two men came to mind. When I returned to work the next morning, my senior lead came and asked me for my selections. After I responded, he looked at me, shocked, and said, "Are you crazy? Of the two guys you picked one is slow and the other is at the bottom of the list of 400 planners!" I said, "Yes, but I believe they are supposed to do the job." "Well, it's your neck!" he said in a somewhat scoffing manner.

What he had not told me the day before was that this assignment actually had two purposes. The first was to re-establish the scrapped plans and tools, which we had to do no matter what, but the second reason was to test my leadership abilities and suitability before being promoted to a lead position.

As I recall, we had one month to complete the project. During this time, I conducted regular status reviews with them as I checked their work and kept track of how each of them was doing both individually and as a team.

One day a small package came for the man rated at the bottom of the list of 400 planners in the organization. It contained a lapel pin honoring him for 20 or 25 years of service to the company. As I talked with him, he indicated that it was difficult for him to receive the pin. He knew the company, in general, appreciated his service, but being at the bottom of the retention rankings and having lived with the stigma of being the least valued employee of over 400 for a number of years was very discouraging to him, especially since no one had ever really tried to help him become something more. Ironically, he was one of the nicest, quietest, and caring people you would ever want to meet, but few people knew that.

He then thanked me for selecting him for the special assignment and trusting him to do a good job. He said no one had ever selected him for a special assignment. As we continued to talk, I saw on his face and heard in his voice a deep appreciation for being valued for who he was and for what God had placed within him. I was fairly good friends with the other man I had selected, but I really did not know this man at all before requesting him for that special assignment. What was the outcome? We finished the project with time to spare, under budget, and with no glitches.

At the end of the project, I realized why God had me select those two men. They both had *gifts* within them that went unnoticed by the organization's management, and He wanted others to see those *gifts* and those men for what He had placed within them.

AS INDIVIDUALS, WHAT ARE WE SUPPOSED TO DO WITH THE *GIFTS* (ABILITIES, TALENTS, AND MOTIVATIONS) GOD HAS GIVEN US?

Some time ago, I wanted to do a project I believed God had been stirring in my heart for a number of years. I knew God had gifted me to do this particular activity, but in an effort to honor those in authority, I chose to request permission to move forward. Before making my request, I had prayed extensively about how to proceed. Then one day during my prayer time, I sensed the Lord say, "You don't have to ask permission." However, because of my desire to honor those in authority, I took that as a suggestion rather than a command. So I made an appointment to talk with each leader and asked permission. My request was turned down.

Several months later a friend said, "I believe you disobeyed God when you asked man's permission. The Lord told you that you didn't need to ask, and the outcome has been that man has stopped you from doing what God had given you to do, and your ability to earn an income has been negatively affected." His reproof struck deep. I realized that *because God gave me the gifts I have, I don't need the permission of man to use those gifts. I already have the authority and approval of God to go forward!*

GIFT CARRIERS

2 Timothy 1:6-7 is an admonition to each of us as a *gift carrier*. Whether you are young or old, male or female, *visionary* or *implementer*; you are not to ignore, stifle, or hide the *gifts* God has given you. He gave them *to you* to fulfill His covenant *with you*, to make room *for you*, and ultimately to make room *for Him* wherever you are and wherever He tells you to go. He wants you to *kindle* them, to *ignite* them, and to cause them to *burn bright* and *become active*. Here's the verse quoted:

> For this reason I remind you to *kindle* afresh *the gift of God which is in you* through the laying on of my hands. For *God has not given* us a spirit of *timidity*, but of power and love and discipline.

Notice the warning: *Do not be timid about it!* The word timid means to lack self-confidence—shy, hesitant, full of anxiety and fear about the future. Timidity is NOT from God.

Notice also that Paul did not tell Timothy to ask anyone's permission to use his gift. While there are times when organizational protocol requires that we ask permission of those in authority, be careful that you do not seek the permission of people to do what God has already given you permission to do—especially if you are not under their direct authority. Depending on the condition of their heart, they may not want the *gift* of God in you! That's right; they may reject you. In fact, I will guarantee that someone somewhere will reject you!! That is a terribly depressing thought, but it is the reality of this world, and we have all participated in that reality at one time or another. However, Jesus' response to such rejection was not to cower in shame and depression. In Matthew 10:37-38, He says *three times*, they are "not worthy of Me." He did not say that out of arrogance or independence. He said it because He knew who He was and the *gift* He was to the world, and He was not timid about sharing Himself as that *gift*. He just stated the truth.

GIFT RECEIVERS

Finally, if you are in the position of being a *gift receiver*, be careful that you are not partial to some and ignore others—especially those that are not just like you or do not fit your preconceived expectations! You very well may be rejecting and dishonoring the *gift* God has sent your way, the one you possibly have been praying that God would send your way!

I close this chapter with James 2:1-10:

> My brethren, do not hold your faith in our glorious Lord Jesus Christ with an attitude of personal favoritism. For if a man comes into your assembly with a gold ring and dressed in fine clothes, and there also comes in a poor man in dirty clothes, and you pay special attention to the one who is wearing the fine clothes, and say, 'You sit here in a good place,' and you say to the poor man, 'You stand over there, or sit down by my footstool,' have you not made distinctions among yourselves, and become judges with evil motives?

> Did not God choose the poor of this world to be rich in faith and heirs of the kingdom which He promised to those who love Him? But you

have dishonored the poor man. Is it not the rich who oppress you and personally drag you into court? Do they not blaspheme the fair name by which you have been called?

If, however, you are fulfilling the royal law according to the Scripture, "YOU SHALL LOVE YOUR NEIGHBOR AS YOURSELF," you are doing well. But if you show partiality, you are committing sin and are convicted by the law as transgressors. For whoever keeps the whole law and yet stumbles in one point, he has become guilty of all.

CHAPTER 8

Every ONE Contributes

*When you assemble, each one has a psalm, has a
teaching, has a revelation, has a tongue, has an
interpretation.
Let all things be done for edification.
1 Corinthians 14:26*

I stumbled across this verse a number of years ago. By *stumbled* I mean that even though I had read it many times during the course of reading my Bible, I had never really *seen* it. Then one day as I was having a quiet time, this verse seemed to jump off the page and confirmed what God had been stirring in my spirit for many years.

I love to learn; and because of my technical gifting, my heart and mind naturally recognize and gravitate toward anything that has a process attached to it. So when I am in a group (usually a church group) for any length of time and sense it's floundering for some unknown reason, I naturally begin to look for why that is happening. Here is what I have learned:

The traditional church model, where the *servant in authority* does all or most of the talking (even in small or home group settings) is contrary to what God tells us to do when we are together. In fact, just the opposite is what God has in mind. Why? Because God gives every <u>ONE</u> something to contribute every time two or more meet together. That's what 1 Corinthians 14:26 says.

In the verses following 1 Corinthians 14:26 (v27-40), the Apostle Paul gives guidelines for church order. These guidelines provide for a few to speak out, in succession, so that confusion does not abound. I am not speaking against maintaining order in a meeting. My point is that God gives each person something to contribute in a meeting for a reason!

Why is every ONE'S contribution so important?

First, *God has something to say through each one of us, and we need to give Him that opportunity if we expect to see Him move in our midst.*

Proverbs 27:17 says, "Iron sharpens iron, so one man sharpens another." *God has designed it so that we learn from one another.* His instruction to speak out is not limited to those who consider themselves 5-fold ministers (apostles, prophets, evangelists, pastors, or teachers) as listed in Ephesians 4. He instructs each one of us to be both a disciple and a discipler, and we learn how to disciple as we sharpen one another by sharing what God is speaking to us about.

As you watch a sword fight, you can hear the swords scrape together as they engage one another. Think how boring it would be if you watched only one person wielding their sword, buffeting nothing but the air! While that might be a good way to practice personal technique, swordsmen are most effective at sharpening their skills when sparring with an opponent.

Second, *giving each ONE a time to demonstrate what God is doing inside of them creates accountability.*

Developing the ability to speak out about what God is doing inside each one of us requires practice. Part of the role of a true *servant in authority* is to ensure that those following them become equipped to be more effective. That holds true whether you are in ministry, business, government, or any facet of family or society. But it takes practice to become effective.

I received a new set of golf clubs for my birthday last year. In one sense, you could say that I am "equipped" to be a great golfer. But merely having the clubs does not make me a golfer; it only makes me the proud owner of a new set of clubs. I need to practice to become a capable golfer. When the scripture talks about equipping others, I do not believe it means to give everyone a "new set of golf clubs." It means to go a step further and help them become proficient at doing all that it takes to become an "effective golfer." True equipping is actually discipleship in its purest form.

Proverbs 16:1 says, "The plans of the heart belong to man, but the answer of the tongue is from the Lord." Practicing the use of our gifts in front of others causes a shift in our hearts to take place. Within us develops a sense of accountability and confirmation of what is really in our hearts. I began to see this in myself during the past few years. There would be one plan in my heart; but when faced with speaking what the Lord was teaching me or saying to me, the answer that rolled off my tongue was different from what seemed to be rolling around in my mind. It was coming from a deeper place within my heart—a place that God had been touching.

Third, as stated in the previous chapter, "A man's gift makes room for him, and brings him before great men" (Proverbs 18:16). *Providing a regular time for each person to share their gift with a group helps prepare them to stand before great men.*

Have you ever stood before a "great man" (or woman) of influence, and then stumbled and stuttered because you did not know what to say? Practicing our gifts in a safe environment will *equip* us to stand before "great men," able to exercise our gift with both skill and confidence.

As a program manager at Boeing, every week I had to present the status of the program I oversaw to vice presidents, directors, and other managers within the division. These were "great men" in that realm. They had an incredible amount of responsibility and authority to make things happen and they could see right through someone who was either afraid or did not know what they were talking about. Had I not had the practice and experience of standing before "great men" in previous lesser assignments, I would have felt intimidated by such an influential crowd.

Finally, *no man, woman, or child can be in a state of true and complete joy until they have take the opportunity to express what is deep inside.* 1st John 1:1-4 summarizes this well:

> What was from the beginning, *what we have heard, what we have seen* with our eyes, *what we have looked at and touched* with our hands, *concerning the Word of Life*—and *the life was*

manifested, and *we have seen and testify and proclaim* to you the eternal life, which was with the Father and was manifested to us—*what we have seen and heard we proclaim* to you also, *so that you too may have fellowship with us;* and indeed our fellowship is with the Father, and with His Son Jesus Christ. *These things we write, so that <u>our joy may be made complete.</u>*

"What we have heard…what we have seen…what we have touched…concerning the Word of Life…we testify and proclaim…so that you too may have fellowship with us…<u>so that our joy may be made complete.</u>"

When we are not given the opportunity to contribute what we have to give, we lose hope and we lose joy. The ability and desire to contribute is placed deep within the heart of each man, woman, and child from the time they are born until the time they die. It is there because God put it there. Taking the time to recognize the gift(s) of each person and giving them an opportunity to share that gift, makes room for them. When there is not room, there is no joy. When there is room, the opportunity to express the gift within makes a person joyful. John even goes so far as to say that it makes joy complete.

When it comes to equipping people to do the work of the ministry, we need to establish a venue in the midst of our regular times together for everyone to practice what God is giving them to share.

I have two examples for you to consider:

A pastor of a church we attended years ago informed a group of about forty men that the men's ministry was once again being jump-started. He invited each one to express what they wanted to see happen in the group. One by one, each gave their response. Many expressed an interest in sports activities and traditional gatherings. I suggested giving each an opportunity, on a rotating basis, to share with the group whatever God had been speaking to him about recently. My rationale was several-fold.

First, because *iron sharpens iron* (Proverbs 27:17) I felt it would be valuable for us, as a group, to become "sharpened" by what God was teaching each man. Personally, I really wanted to hear and be "sharpened" by what God was speaking to each man. I also needed and wanted their help to become skilled in that ability myself.

Second, I felt it would be valuable for us all to work together to raise each other up, learning how to become effective *servants in authority*, positions we held in our homes but were not trained to carry out effectively. I was hearing things from God on a regular basis, but I struggled with certain aspects of being a husband, father, and messenger of God.

Third, I had a strong desire to see men, including myself, be discipled and not just entertained. The words disciple and discipline come from the same Latin root *discipulus*, meaning pupil. A true disciple wants to develop discipline, which requires practice, not just listening to someone else.

Fourth, many of the men did not necessarily appear sad, but they were quiet, reserved, and seemed to lack joy. Even when asked one-on-one, few of them really had much to say about what God was saying to them or was doing in their lives. I believe that was the result of them rarely being challenged with expressing what God was doing in them and through them before "great men." They had become like Moses in a way, lacking eloquence (Exodus 4:10) and not able to talk much about anything except work.

Unfortunately, the pastor's response was quite negative, opting instead for the "I talk, you listen" approach. So the men's ministry became a series of sports related activities with an occasional Saturday breakfast and a few retreats, always with the same traditional few key people doing all the talking. What the pastor missed, however, was the opportunity to challenge forty men and raise them up into their destinies with God, equipped to "stand before great men" and speak confidently about what God was doing in them and through them.

The second and contrasting example happened a few years later in a venue that focused on training and equipping. The teacher's subject for the week was "Walking in the Spirit." Toward the end of the week, we arrived at class and began to settle in for another lecture. The instructor welcomed us and told us to place our notebooks against the wall, take down the tables, and put the chairs in a circle. He then proceeded to tell us we were going to have church, 1 Corinthians 14 style. I admit I was a bit afraid, having absolutely no grid for his approach or what was about to happen.

We sat in a large circle (there were about sixty of us), and he gave the group two simple instructions: First, listen for whatever the Holy Spirit tells you. Second, do whatever He tells you to do. There was dead silence for the first few minutes, which felt like an eternity; then one woman began to sing, another danced, someone else read a scripture, and another spoke whatever the Spirit gave them to say. One by one, every person participated.

I don't recall what I did. However, at the end of the next two hours, I remember feeling like Jello; and I think I was laying on the floor, unable to get up for some time. The amazing thing, however, was that EVERY <u>ONE</u> CONTRIBUTED; and the results were powerful for the entire group without there being any chaos or confusion.

In closing, I believe ministries typically flounder because there is rarely a place given for each ONE to exercise his/her gifts and testify of the revelations God has given them.   Until that turns around, I do not expect that many people will be raised up to be all God intends them to be. Merely providing that atmosphere, however, is not going to be the greatest challenge. The greatest challenge will be making it a safe atmosphere—where each one can learn by trial and error without risk of criticism, ridicule, or alienation.

Servants in Authority: Are you willing to loosen the reigns of control and let God speak through the least of those in your care?

Every ONE else: Are you willing to contribute?

CHAPTER 9

The True Mission of the 5-Fold Minister

He gave some as apostles, and some as prophets, and
some as evangelists, and some as pastors and teachers,
for the equipping of the saints for the work of service,
to the building up of the body of Christ;
until we all attain to the unity of the faith, and of the
knowledge of the Son of God, to a mature man, to the
measure of the stature which belongs to the fullness of
Christ.
Ephesians 4:11-13

In September of 2007, I had the privilege of sitting in on a strategic planning workshop being held for ministry *servants in authority*. During the 3-day seminar, principles were taught to each group that were designed to help them see the connections between their personal and organizational histories, inherited character and gifting traits, testimonies and prophecies, and how they could be used together to define vision and mission for their organizations. Everyone got a lot out of the teachings and exercises, but one group really struggled with converting their discoveries into a comprehensive mission statement that truly reflected the heart of the pastor and his team.

I watched as the group of twelve laboriously analyzed the 200+ sticky notes adhered to the flip-chart pages posted on the wall that contained the results of almost 3 days worth of work. As they struggled, I began to pray quietly for them. I saw and sensed their frustration and was asking God to reveal His answer for them. As I sat and observed their process, one of their elders asked for my help. After asking a few questions to refine their focus, I decided to review their responses documented on the vast number of sticky notes on the wall. As I read, I prayed. I was asking God to reveal a simple, straightforward mission statement that clearly captured the true heart-cry of this team. After a few minutes, the senior pastor joined me near the wall, and then my eyes caught something on one particular sticky note that prompted me to say to the senior pastor...

"Your mission is to recognize, raise up, and release people into their God-given destiny."

He exclaimed, "That's it! That's it!! THAT is our mission: To *recognize, raise up, and release people into their God-given destinies."*

I got excited because his heart resonated with what God had been showing me for several years. Yet, I had not had the exact words to articulate it until that moment. It was not just his breakthrough; it was my breakthrough as well.

In Chapter 5, I talked about how the gifts of the Son (His giving of apostles, prophets, evangelists, pastors, and teachers) are actually a promotion of those children of God that faithfully invested their lives developing the *gifts* they received from the Father and the

Holy Spirit to become *equippers* of the next generation. When I declared that statement to that team, this dedicated pastor clearly saw his current assignment as an *equipper* in the Body of Christ…and his mission was to *recognize, raise up,* and then *release* people God brought to their church into their God-given destinies.

I believe that is the one and only true mission of those that consider themselves "5-fold ministers." Why? To *equip* means to *train*—to supply with the tools, provisions, and qualities necessary for performance. Proverbs 22:6 says, *"Train* up a child in the way he should go, even when he is old he will not depart from it."

You cannot effectively *equip* someone to succeed without taking time to do these three process steps:

1. *Recognize* their existing gifts, skills, yearnings, and limitations;

2. *Raise them up* by helping them to develop and effectively use their strengths and overcome their weaknesses; and then

3. *Release* them into their own Great Commission assignment, as revealed by God.

Notice that the process is not complete until you *release* them.

Does the Bible reflect this process? I believe so.

When Jesus began His ministry and chose the 12 disciples, He saw what God the Father had placed in each one—the gifts and the shortcomings. He knew who would betray and deny Him. He knew who was zealous and who doubted everything except what they could personally touch. He *recognized* what He had to work with.

During the next three years He discipled them, helping them develop their strengths and eliminate their weaknesses, so they would be prepared to fulfill the commission He would bestow on them before returning to heaven. He *raised them up*. During this *raising up* period, Jesus sent them on a "mini-Great Commission" assignment (John 10:1-29). The sending of the seventy disciples was a practice run—part of their preparation. Then just before He ascended to heaven, Jesus gave them His authority and their assignment—to go and make disciples of all nations. He *released* them.

At this point you might be wondering, "How do I *recognize, raise up, and release*? Let's take a closer look at each element.

HOW CAN YOU *RECOGNIZE* THE GIFTS, SKILLS, YEARNINGS, AND LIMITATIONS A PERSON CARRIES?

One way to facilitate that is to use any combination of tests and other communication tools that are available, many of which include a variety of questions asked from different perspectives. Such tests are helpful in identifying a person's interests and gifting at the time they take the test. They can even identify some life-long traits. There are a number of good tests out there and I personally have taken many of them. Depending on your own personality, some report formats might be easier for you to understand and relate to than others. Either way, I believe such tests can be used to help *servants in authority* and individuals recognize their existing gifts, skills, yearnings, and limitations.

But probably the most important activity you can do to *recognize* what a person carries is to just talk with them. Invest time in getting to know them. Being and feeling heard is what everyone needs and wants. Give them your undivided attention. Take time to really listen, and do it on a regular basis. Their strengths and weaknesses will not all be revealed to you during one 30-minute interview; they will become most evident over the course of time and in the midst of meaningful activities. Believe it or not, you taking time getting to know them is actually "doing the work" of the ministry.

As you become aware of their gifts, skills, yearnings, and limitations; the *equipper* in you will begin to see what you need to do to facilitate their growth—what you need to do to *raise them up*.

Here is an example that illustrates what I mean.

When I was a manufacturing planner, I had the privilege of working for a supervisor that lived by several very strict core values; one of which was to always "train his replacement." That core value was so important to him that he required every person serving in a managerial role within his organization to do the same.

When he became our manager, he and I seemed to instantly connect for some reason. I do not recall why because we were exact opposites in many ways. Maybe our contrasts complimented one another. Anyway, I always enjoyed our talks and his open-door policy encouraged one-on-one time with him, which everyone respected and did not abuse.

As part of his process for *equipping* me to become eligible for promotion to the position of lead planner, he gave me an assignment: I was to write several letters for his signature. Once complete, each would go to a significant number of managers and organizations, establishing or enforcing one or more department policies on the projects for which he was responsible. He gave clear instructions on what he expected and then released me to complete the project.

At the time, I believed my letter writing skills were very good. I was technical, thorough, and very specific in my use of words to avoid double meanings. A few days later, I submitted my initial drafts for his review. Within a short few hours, I received them back with numerous red edits. We went through this process four times. When I received the letters back for the fifth time, still with one or two minor corrections, I got very frustrated. Quite honestly, I felt like he was nitpicking my letters to death!

As I walked into his office, I huffed and puffed a little and then expressed my frustration regarding the continual minor corrections. (He and I got along very well, so my demeanor did not bother him at all.) I placed the letters on his desk and said, "Maybe you should just write them yourself!"

I will never forget his response. He sat back in his chair, grinning, and said, *"I'm trying to teach you how to represent me.* And in order for you to represent me, you need to be able to write in a way that reflects my style; how I would personally speak and respond." He then went on to explain that this process was just one of many I would encounter while I worked for him, and that the process was intended to train me for promotion; possibly even to replace him.

His response spoke volumes; so much so, that now I intentionally seek to "train my replacement" in every work assignment I am given.

What was he doing? During the many meetings we had in his office, he was *recognizing* who I was and what was inside of me. He was taking inventory of what I had and what I lacked. As my time under his management progressed, he gave me other specific assignments within the course of my normal work responsibilities. These assignments were to *raise me up*, to *equip* me to do greater things. They helped to strengthen my strengths and overcome my weaknesses. Finally, after having spent several years under his wing, he *released* me to work on developing a new commercial jetliner—an assignment that resulted in my promotion into management.

Clearly, Ephesians 4:11-13 (the title verses of this chapter) are verses for the Church, but I also believe similarly gifted people have God-given assignments in business, medicine, and every other part of society. Not so much to equip people to become ministers of the Gospel to fulfill Jesus' mandate in Matthew 28, but to raise up their successors by equipping them to serve effectively in whatever job or capacity they are called. The senior pastor of the church we attend often reminds us that our spiritual ceiling, the highest level we have been able to attain to personally, is supposed to be the floor of our children so they do not have to repeat our mistakes. Should that not also be true outside the four walls of the church?

So, whether you are a homemaker or work outside the home in some other capacity, you have an assignment to equip others. That includes your children, your subordinates, and those called to serve alongside you in some capacity. It is actually part of your progressive training; part of YOUR training to someday be promoted by Jesus to the role of *senior equipper* as an apostle, prophet, evangelist, pastor, or teacher—one of His most trusted *servants with authority*! And here is some great news for you: You don't have to wait until you are old to learn how to *recognize, raise up* and *release* those around you.

In closing, I would like to quote two passages that I hope encourage you to become a true *equipper*.

Philippians 2:3-4:

> Do nothing from selfishness or empty conceit, but with humility of mind regard one another as more important than yourselves; do not merely look out for your own personal interests, but also for the interests of others.

And Matthew 20:26-28:

> Whoever wishes to become great among you shall be your servant, and whoever wishes to be first among you shall be your slave; just as the Son of Man did not come to be served, but to serve, and to give His life a ransom for many.

CHAPTER 10

Working Together

Masters, grant to your slaves justice and
fairness, knowing that you too have a
Master in heaven.
Colossians 4:1

*W*orking Together was a slogan we had at Boeing for several years. The intention was to foster a prolonged sense of teamwork because we were "all in 'this' together." From the perspective of our Board of Directors and senior management team, our ability to "work together" would largely determine our success or failure to achieve the program goals, which directly affected the company's stock value and our customer's satisfaction level with our products and services.

Personally, I thought it was a great slogan, as slogans go, because it pointed us toward a target that included, or at least implied, mutual respect and honor. However, conflicting organizational agendas and priorities at times led some managers to set aside their commitment to *work together* in order to maintain their own performance goals (which affected their year-end bonus), even when doing so meant other organizations suffered greatly. The following story illustrates what I mean.

We had just begun final assembly production on three new derivatives of the same aircraft model. The final assembly factory personnel were already working overtime to meet a very aggressive production schedule designed to meet the contracted delivery dates of the airplanes. However, they had one problem. The business unit that designed and manufactured all of the wiring harnesses and electrical systems for the aircraft was not finished with the design work, resulting in the final assembly factory not having some of the electrical assemblies they needed to maintain the production schedule.

During a production review meeting, a management representative from the electrical business unit was giving the Final Assembly Director of Manufacturing a detailed status report on the problem. He reported that they were behind schedule because they lacked a sufficient number of designers to do the work, but they were not in the process of adding more designers or working additional overtime because doing so would cause them to exceed their initial budget ceiling. The disappointment in the room was great, and the Director of Manufacturing put it all into perspective when he essentially said, "So the final assembly business unit is failing to meet their production schedule because the electrical business unit won't do what it takes to meet theirs." The answer from the management representative was, "Yes."

The story above is an excellent example of NOT *working together*. But what does it take to establish a *working together* atmosphere? I believe there are several principles we need to establish and judiciously follow.

First

Commit to doing everything within your power to help others succeed—even if it is not to your own benefit.

In the story above, the final assembly business unit was an "internal customer" of the electrical business unit. It was "internal" because they were both part of the same division within the company. However, their collective success (or failure) had a direct impact on the company's most important external customers—the airlines awaiting delivery of their new airplanes.

In Psalm 15, David talks about the kind of character it takes to have integrity and abide with God. The last part of verse 4 says, "He swears to his own hurt, and does not change." Philippians 2:3-4 tells us that being so concerned about our own success that those around us are unable to succeed is "selfishness and empty conceit." James 3:14 goes on to describe *selfish ambition* as "earthly, natural, and demonic." In a true *working together* atmosphere, everyone is dedicated to doing whatever it takes to help EVERYONE succeed. There are no prima donnas and there are no "one-man shows."

Second

Establish and maintain an atmosphere of forgiveness.

Romans 3:23 says, "All have sinned and fall short of the glory of God." Everyone makes mistakes; and while it might be extremely difficult at times to forgive, or even forget, the insensitivity, abuse, arrogance, or ignorance of a co-worker or boss; unforgiveness will eventually breed bitterness and mistrust. Both will make working together difficult, if not impossible. Let me give you an example from my own experience.

I sat in a meeting of about 30 manufacturing planners and tool engineers shortly after beginning a new assignment on a new airplane model that was being designed at Boeing. As a result of my experience as a program manager during the previous few years, I was invited to join the program and was considered one of the few "experts" of the new process the team had been directed to implement on this particular airplane program. It was the same process I helped develop during my previous assignment. During the meeting, one particular female tool designer seemed to have a huge "chip" on her shoulder. She challenged and criticized everything I said. No matter how hard I tried to maintain a positive, "working-together" attitude, I eventually reacted to her in a way that was not wholly appropriate.

Immediately, I sensed a negative shift in the atmosphere of the meeting, which I knew was not good for the team. Words have power and once they are released, they can't be taken back. That evening, I felt convicted about the way I had responded to this particular co-worker. Although she was gruff and abrasive, I knew I had truly hurt her in some way. But since I did not know her personally, I really did not know what damage I had done.

The next morning I knew I needed to apologize to her, so I went to her desk and asked if we could talk. She seemed quite nervous and unsure of why I was there. Without addressing her attitude from the day before, I confessed that I felt my comments to her during the meeting were inappropriate and asked her to forgive me. She stared at me and then replied, "Yes." She seemed ready to cry, and was not at all interested in talking with me, so I thanked her and went back to my cubicle. The net result was that our subsequent team meetings were much more amicable.

Third
Let kindness emanate from you and appreciate it when it comes from others. Kindness is actually a gift from God Himself.

In writing to the Romans, Paul asked, "Do you think lightly of the riches of His *kindness* and tolerance and patience, not knowing that the *kindness* of God leads you to repentance (Romans 2:4)?" We must never take genuine kindness for granted because genuine kindness is actually a gift from God. And when it is expressed through the people around us, it is evidence of His tolerance and patience with each one of us. Because the kindness of God leads people to repentance, genuine kindness and forgiveness work hand-in-hand to help establish an atmosphere that invites the presence of the Holy Spirit—an atmosphere that makes it easier to receive Spirit-led strategies.

Is there strife and tension within your business or ministry team? As a *servant in authority*, you need to take the initiative to ask forgiveness for whatever your part may have been. Repentance is not a sign of weakness, but of strength, and doing so will release forgiveness and kindness to others and make it easier for your team to *work together*.

Fourth
Render service to one another with good will.

Ephesians 6:7-9, says, "With *good will* render service, as to the Lord, and not to men, knowing that whatever good thing each one does, this he will receive back from the Lord...and masters, do the same...give up threatening, knowing that both their Master and yours is in heaven, and there is no partiality with Him."

What is "good will"?

"Good will" is similar, but different, to the business term "goodwill" used to describe the intangible asset businesses have in the existence of a loyal, repeat customer base; the people that not only like to do business with them, but actually choose to do business with them as opposed to someone else.

The American Heritage Dictionary defines our *will* as, "The mental faculty by which one deliberately chooses or decides upon a course of action."

So to operate with "good will" means that we deliberately choose to do what is good (positive or desirable) rather than what is bad. But how do we determine what is "good?" Fortunately, Ephesians 6:7 also defines "good" as being whatever is "as to the Lord." So our measure for "good" is whatever God defines as "good."

To paraphrase, Paul says we are to serve one another with kindness, friendliness, and willingness to agree without protest. Also, notice that he gives that instruction specifically to both those **under** authority and those **in** authority. Why? Because God is the Father of all; Jesus is our only Leader; and those that have been given authority on this earth will be held accountable to both **our** Father in heaven and **our** Leader sitting at His right hand. He alone will be the decider of what we have done that is "good."

Fifth
Give people a chance.

There are many people hungry for a chance to prove themselves, not to earn the favor of man, but because deep in their heart they burn with a passion to use their gifts, either as a *visionary* or an *implementer*. They are anxious for an opportunity. From what I have seen and personally experienced, the passion a person has to use the *gifts* they have been given by God, IS God's Spirit moving within them. Therefore, I believe the most significant test for a *servant in authority* is not how effective they are at saying "No," but rather what they are willing to do in order to be able to say "Yes." Remember, the true call of every 5-fold minister and *servant in authority* is to **recognize, raise up, and release** people into their God-given destinies. That takes risk—risk to say "Yes."

In Isaiah 6:8 the prophet Isaiah wrote, "I heard the voice of the Lord, saying, 'Whom shall I send, and who will go for Us?' Then I said, 'Here am I, send me.' And He said, 'Go.'"

God said, "Go" to Isaiah because Isaiah was willing, not because he was the most gifted, the most qualified, or had the most charisma. If God was willing to take a chance on sending Isaiah, and Jesus was willing to take a chance on sending the disciples, shouldn't every *servant in authority* also be willing to give the people they are called to serve a chance to prove themselves? I believe so, and I believe God says so too.

Are there exceptions? Absolutely. It would obviously be unwise to say "yes" to anyone that has proven to be untrustworthy and/or unsafe, especially when it comes to working with other people, including children. And it would obviously not be wise to say "yes" to someone who was not even remotely qualified for the work that needed to be accomplished (e.g. sending someone with no medical training to perform medical procedures).

My point is this—if, as a *servant in authority*, someone comes and asks you for a chance and you have no reason to <u>not</u> trust them (they have a known positive track record of integrity), give them a chance to prove themselves—not just for their sake, but for yours as well. Why? Because you, as a *servant in authority*, will never be wholly effective at **recognizing, raising up, and releasing** the next generation of *servants in authority* unless you are willing to give people a chance.

I have heard some leaders talk about being *"fathers"* to those they oversee. Even though Jesus instructs us to never call anyone *"father"* (Matthew 23:9), those with authority can serve with the heart of our Father in heaven by providing an atmosphere that gives people a chance to learn, which includes trying and possibly failing, then trying again and succeeding. Jesus said that we are to "disciple all nations." We cannot disciple people without being willing to give them a chance to prove what they are capable of accomplishing.

At this point you might be asking, "What if they make a mistake?" Here is some freeing news for you. They will! And some of those mistakes might be very serious, causing embarrassment, physical harm, or financial loss—not just to them, but also to you! But remember, it's not about you. It's about them. The only part that is really about you is whether you can pass the test to **recognize, raise up, and release** them into all that God has for them; to equip them to go farther than you have ever been!

Proverbs 14:4 says, "Where no oxen are, the manger is clean, but much revenue comes by the strength of the ox." What is this verse really saying? Before motorized tractors, farmers used teams of oxen to pull the wagons, plows, and other farm tools they used to be productive. But to benefit from the oxen, the farmer had to be willing to clean his barn of what the oxen deposited there on a daily basis. (I'm sure you get the picture.) People learning to use their *gifts* are like oxen in the sense that they make mistakes (messes) that need to be "cleaned up." And *cleaning up* is part of the process of *raising up*.

1 Thessalonians 5:14-15 summarizes well the essence of the five points noted above and what is expected of all *servants in authority*.

> We urge you, brethren, admonish *(caution)* the unruly, encourage *(inspire)* the fainthearted, help *(assist)* the weak, be patient *(endure with calmness)* with everyone. See that no one repays another with evil for evil, but always seek after that which is good for one another and for all people.

CHAPTER 11

Stumbling Blocks to *Servants in Authority*

It is inevitable that stumbling blocks should come,
but woe to him through whom they come!
It would be better for him if a millstone were hung
around his neck and he were thrown into the sea, than
that he should cause one of these little ones to stumble.
Luke 17:1-2

Stumbling blocks. In Luke 17 Jesus told His disciples that "stumbling blocks" were inevitable and then warned them that there would be consequences for the person through whom they came.

The Greek word used for "stumbling blocks" in Luke 17:1-2 is *skandalon*. It means "offense," and offenses become hindrances to people, keeping them from becoming all God meant for them to be. In this chapter, we will look at the list of offenses mentioned in James 3 and Matthew 23 that greatly hinder people. At the top of the list are the hindrances of *jealousy* and *selfish ambition*. But in order to understand *selfish* ambition, we need to first define *ambition*.

The American Heritage Dictionary defines *ambition* as "an eager or strong desire to achieve something, such as fame or power."

Ambition is an amazing asset for *visionaries* and *implementers* alike. It is something we all need in order to move forward in life. When you really think about it, it takes some degree of *ambition* to accomplish virtually anything, although we typically attribute the need for *ambition* to accomplish projects or goals that require significant amounts of personal or group effort and time. No one would argue that it takes *ambition* to get a college degree, start and grow a business, or be a great parent. And it certainly takes *ambition* to grow in God and walk with Him all the days of our lives.

So, if *ambition* is necessary for accomplishment, is *ambition* always good?

Just as with everything else, *ambition* has both a normal and abnormal use (abuse), and when used abnormally, it becomes a *"stumbling block."* James addresses the issue of *selfish ambition* in James 3:13-18. He says…

> Who among you is wise and understanding? Let him show by his good behavior his deeds in the gentleness of wisdom. But if you have **bitter jealousy** and **selfish ambition** in your heart, do not be arrogant and so lie against the truth. This wisdom is not that which comes down from above, but is **earthly, natural, demonic.** For **where jealousy and selfish ambition exist, there is disorder and every evil thing.** But the wisdom from above is first pure, then peaceable, gentle, reasonable, full of mercy

and good fruits, unwavering, without hypocrisy. And the seed whose fruit is righteousness is sown in peace by those who make peace.

Notice that *bitter jealousy* and *selfish ambition* are listed together; and that they are both classified as *earthly, natural, and demonic; breeding disorder and every evil thing.* I believe they are mentioned together because *jealousy* **breeds** *selfish ambition.* What is jealousy? It is the fear of losing affection or position, of being displaced, or supplanted by another. Everyone wants to be needed and wanted, and if our *gift* is supposed to make room for us, then the fear of our *gifts* being rejected can cause us to become *jealous* of the success of another and do just about anything to make sure we don't lose our place. Consequently, we all have the potential to fall into the trap of *selfish ambition.*

In Matthew 20:25-28, Jesus told His disciples about the *selfish ambitions* of the Gentile rulers and the effects their ambitions had on the people. He then contrasted their ambitions with His own. He came to serve; not to be served. A few chapters later, in Matthew 23, Jesus continued His comments but the venue had moved from a private setting with just the disciples and a few of their family members to a public gathering that also included the religious leaders, scribes and Pharisees, and many men, women, and children.

Jesus was particularly disappointed and grieved with one specific group of people in His day, and it was not the sinners sitting on the hillside listening to Him. He came down hard on the scribes and the Pharisees, the spiritual leaders who were supposed to be **servants in authority.** Why was He so directly and openly critical of them? Why did they grieve Him so much?

He was critical of the scribes and the Pharisees of the day because they misrepresented the heart of God to the people. Jesus very specifically describes how that was happening in Matthew 23. In fact, He was so concerned about it that He did not bother holding a private meeting behind closed doors to avoid offending these religious leaders. He spoke about it in the open with everyone who was within earshot—the scribes, the Pharisees, His disciples, and numerous other men, women, and children—people whom He knew were His Father's gifts to the world. I can think of only one reason why He chose to do that—because Jesus, the Father, and the Holy Spirit did not like being misrepresented to the people and wanted everyone to hear the same message at the same time. There was no mistaking God's perspective on the matter.

So what were the problems Jesus addressed—the *stumbling blocks* of *servants in authority* that He felt so compelled to warn everyone about? They were all rooted in *jealousy* and *selfish ambition*. Let's take a close look at Matthew 23. Notice that Jesus begins by addressing the crowds and His disciples first.

JESUS ADDRESSES THE CROWDS

Pharisaism Exposed (Matthew 23:1-7)

Then Jesus spoke to the crowds and to His disciples, saying: "The scribes and the Pharisees *have seated themselves* in the chair of Moses (of authority); therefore all that they tell you, do and observe, but do not do according to their deeds; for *they say things and do not do them.* They tie up heavy burdens and lay them on men's shoulders, but they themselves are unwilling to move them with so much as a finger. But *they do all their deeds to be noticed by men*; for they broaden their phylacteries and lengthen the tassels of their garments. *They love the place of honor* at banquets and the chief seats in the synagogues, *and respectful greetings* in the market places, *and being called Rabbi by men."*

In other words, Jesus was saying to the people that scribes and Pharisees...

1. Seat themselves in positions of authority

2. Are hypocrites—teaching or saying one thing, but doing the opposite

3. Do deeds to be noticed by others

4. Love places of honor, respectful greetings, and being called "teacher" by men

That was just His introduction. Jesus then instructs the disciples and the crowd with three "Do Nots" and one "Do," clearly still referring to Pharisaism (Matthew 23:8-11).

1. *DO NOT call yourself or anyone else "teacher."* We are all brothers and sisters and we have only one true Teacher, the Holy Spirit (v8).

2. *DO NOT call yourself or anyone else "father."* We have only one true Father, our Creator, and He is in heaven (v9).

3. *DO NOT call yourself or anyone else a "leader."* We have only one true Leader, and that is Jesus Christ (v10).

4. *DO call yourselves servants,* and know that the greatest among you shall be the greatest at serving others (v11).

Jesus instructs His disciples and followers **not to speak or act as these religious leaders acted.** Then He ends his instructions to the crowd with verse 12, "Whoever exalts himself shall be humbled; and whoever humbles himself shall be exalted."

JESUS ADDRESSES THE RELIGIOUS LEADERS

After talking to the crowd, He turns back to address the scribes and Pharisees to express the Father's heart of deep sorrow and dismay over their attitudes and actions. He speaks the truth in the form of eight "woes" (Matthew 23:13-36).

1. *Woe to you...hypocrites...you shut off the kingdom of heaven from people* (v13).

2. *Woe to you...hypocrites...you devour widows' houses, and for a pretense (action intended to deceive) you make long prayers* (v14).

3. *Woe to you...hypocrites...you travel around on sea and land to make one proselyte; and when he becomes one, you make him twice as much a son of hell as yourselves* (v15).

4. *Woe to you, blind guides, who say, "Whoever swears by the temple, that is*

nothing; but whoever swears by the gold of the temple is obligated" (v16).

5. *Woe to you...hypocrites...you tithe...and have neglected the weightier provisions of the law: justice and mercy and faithfulness* (v23).

6. *Woe to you...hypocrites...you clean the outside...but inside...are full of robbery and self-indulgence* (v25).

7. *Woe to you...hypocrites...you...outwardly appear righteous to men, but inwardly you are full of hypocrisy and lawlessness* (v27).

8. *Woe to you...hypocrites...you testify against yourselves* (v29).

"Woe" in the Greek (ouai) is a primary exclamation of grief. Grief is an intense, deep, profound sorrow. Why did Jesus express such grief over and over—eight times, to be exact? **His heart was breaking** over the condition of the religious leaders' hearts. He addressed the leaders as "hypocrites" and "blind guides," describing the specific ways their hearts did not reflect the heart of His Father.

JESUS ADDRESSES EVERYONE

Finally, in Matthew 23:34-36, **Jesus told everyone what He planned to do** about what He had observed during His 33 years on earth.

I am sending you prophets and wise men and scribes; some of them you will kill and crucify, and some of them you will *scourge* in your synagogues, and *persecute* from city to city, so that **upon you may fall the guilt of all the righteous blood shed on earth**, from the blood of righteous Abel to the blood of Zechariah, the son of Berechiah, whom you murdered between the temple and the altar. Truly I say to you, **all these things will come upon this generation.**

Jesus then ends His time with the crowd with an outcry of lament over Jerusalem (Matthew 23:37-39).

Jerusalem, Jerusalem, who **kills** the prophets **and stones those who are sent to her**! How often I wanted to gather your children together, the way a hen gathers her chicks under her wings, and you were unwilling. Behold, your house is being left to you desolate! For I say to you, *from now on you will not see Me until you say, 'BLESSED IS HE WHO COMES IN THE NAME OF THE LORD!"*

I believe Jesus' heart broke over His pronouncement of impending judgment upon His people. In essence, I believe He was saying, "Woe to those who silence God's gifts, God's message, God's people, and God's kingdom. If you do not embrace them, you will not see Me until you acknowledge My coming."

EXERCISING OUR AUTHORITY

As *servants in authority*, how can we help each other avoid tripping over the "stumbling blocks" of attitude and action described by Jesus? I suggest we remember and take to heart the following:

- *Remember where our authority comes from.* God is the only one who grants authority. Even Jesus said to Pilate, "You have no authority over Me unless it had been given you from above" (John 19:11). Therefore, we must remember that any authority we have comes from Him.

- *Use our authority to serve others.* God gives us authority so we may serve and help others become what God intends THEM to be, not so others can serve us (Luke 9:1-2).

- *Use our authority to initiate honor.* The best way to teach honor is to honor others first, not by requiring them to honor us (1 Peter 2:17).

- *Pass the test of embracing God's gifts.* God evaluates those in authority by the way they receive those whom He sends (Matthew 23).

Have you ever read the story of Hophni and Phineas beginning in 1 Samuel 2? Verse 12 says, **"They did not recognize the Lord's authority."** They were the sons of Eli, the chief priest, and they served as the Lord's priests to the people, only they were very wicked and selfish men. Whenever anyone was making a sacrifice at the temple, they would use a three-pronged fork and take whatever they could of the person's sacrifice for themselves, forcibly if necessary. In verse 22 it says they would also have sex with the women stationed at the entrance to the tent of meeting. Unfortunately, Eli's sons would not listen when he tried to correct them; so the Lord withdrew His favor and pronounced judgment on Eli's household and entire family line.

As I recalled that story recently, it struck me that the pieces of "meat" Hophni and Phineas took from the people were examples of the ideas, inventions, and *gifts* that God gives His children in the course of their work or ministry. I have seen similar actions by authority figures in years past. Some with *selfish ambitions* would assume full credit for the work of a peer or subordinate, resulting in them achieving their personal ambitions at the expense of those they were supposed to be serving and equipping. As with God's assessment and judgment regarding the behavior of Hophni and

Phineas, such things disturb God because He expects to be reflected in those to whom He gives positions of authority.

Jesus said, "Follow Me." While we live on earth, we must deal with the realities of this earthly kingdom. However, we get to choose which kingdom's rules we will live by—the rules of this world (selfish ambition) or the rules of the kingdom of heaven (being a servant of all). Jesus came to serve, not to be served; to raise people up, not hold them back. In like manner, we are here to use the *gifts* God gave us to serve others and to help them achieve their potential. Jesus railed on the Pharisees because they were more concerned about being served than about serving those over whom they had authority. He warns us strongly to not be like them.

Which atmosphere do you believe would be more conducive to receiving Spirit-led directions and strategies? One that is filled with *servant-ambition* or one filled with *selfish-ambition?* I think the answer is obvious.

CHAPTER 12

Beware of the Thief

The thief comes only to steal and kill and destroy;
I came that they may have life, and have it abundantly.
John 10:10

Have you ever been robbed? I was. Not at gunpoint or by a mugger, but one night my car was broken into while I was visiting friends in another state. I had not yet made a personal commitment to God. Yet over the course of several months, He had been speaking to me through a variety of circumstances—obviously trying to get my attention. This particular evening He spoke again, but I didn't understand it was Him.

I started out on a trip from California to Washington, D.C. in the summer of 1976. I had just graduated from college and thought it would be fun to go to our nation's bicentennial celebration. I never got there. After driving alone for 1,000 miles in 22 hours, I decided I did not really want to do another 6,000 miles; so I chose instead to turn back and visit friends in Portland, Oregon. After sleeping for four hours in a motel north of Denver, Colorado, I drove non-stop to Portland instead of continuing east.

As I went to bed my first night in Portland, I could see my car parked on the street in front of my friend's house. For some reason, I felt uneasy about leaving my car parked on the street. But my friend and his family had already gone to bed, so I brushed off my concerns as being a little paranoid. When I awoke the next morning, I looked out the window and noticed my passenger door was ajar. My heart sank. I ran down stairs to see what had happened and found most of my belongings that I had left in my car were gone forever. That was one of the times during a several month period in 1976 that I concluded my reticence the night before was actually the Lord warning me to "beware of the thief."

This chapter, however, is not about the kind of thief that steals your possessions. So if you answered "no" to the robbery question, you might want to re-think your answer. I want to talk about another kind of thief, the kind Jesus refers to in the Gospel of John.

During my many years of walking with God, I have heard countless sermons and declarations from church and business *servants in authority*, friends, family, and even myself, saying that Satan is the thief Jesus referred to in John 10:10. I don't know if everyone actually arrived at that conclusion via personal study, or if we all just blindly agreed with the first person we heard make that statement because it sounded good and made sense. Either way, I believe we all arrived at the wrong conclusion. Just like when you found out there was no Easter Bunny or Santa Claus, you need to know that we have all been mistaken. The real thief is NOT Satan! Who was Jesus speaking of?

If you were to read chapters 9 through 12 of the Gospel of John in one sitting you would see who the real thief is. Let's look first at some key verses from John chapter 9:

- John 9:16 says there was division among the Pharisees about Jesus' deity because He had just healed a blind man on the Sabbath.

- The Pharisees "had already agreed that if anyone confessed Him to be the Messiah, he was to be put out of the synagogue" (v22).

- They then asked the former blind man to explain again how he got his eyesight (v24 and 26).

- When he does explain, they revile him saying, "You are His disciple; but we are disciples of Moses" (v28).

- Finally, the Pharisees, being offended at the man's responses, put him out of the synagogue (v34).

- After hearing the former blind man was no longer welcome in the place of worship, Jesus went to find the man to assure him that he had just encountered the kingdom of heaven (v35-39).

In chapter 9, we see the Pharisees offended at the works and words of Jesus and, hence, their rejection of the kingdom of heaven in their midst. They did not receive God's *gift* of Jesus to the world, nor did they approve of others partaking of the *gift*.

Now let's look at chapter 10.

- In John 10:8 Jesus says, "ALL who came before Me are thieves and robbers." Notice the word "all." That is an important word because He is not referring to just one person or being. He is referring to many. He is talking about people who came before Him, not a fallen angel created by God.

- Jesus says, "He who is a hireling...not the owner of the sheep, beholds the wolf coming...and flees...the wolf snatches them, and scatters them" (v12).

- "He flees because he is a hireling, and is not concerned about the sheep" (v13).

In chapter 10, we see that thieves, robbers, and hirelings care more about themselves than anyone else. Because they are not the true/real shepherds, when they see danger approaching they run to protect their own interests. They are not concerned for the lives of the sheep in their care.

Lastly, let's jump to John, chapters 11 and 12 to look at another passage of scripture, one that I am sure you are familiar with. It is the story of Jesus raising Lazarus from the dead.

- In John 11:38-46, Jesus showed up several days after Lazarus had been dead and buried. After instructing the people to move the stone that covered Lazarus' tomb He thanked His Father in heaven for hearing Him and then he cried out with a loud voice, "Lazarus, come forth." Lazarus then came forth, still bound by his burial wrappings.

- Once Lazarus was unbound many began to believe in Jesus and that He manifested the kingdom of heaven, which provoked the chief priests and Pharisees to conspire to kill Jesus (John 11:47-57). But they didn't stop there.

- John 12:11 says, "The chief priests planned to put Lazarus to death also; because on account of him many of the Jews were going away and were believing in Jesus."

In chapters 11 and 12, the religious leaders covertly plotted to kill Jesus to destroy the works of God. But they knew killing Him would not be enough. They needed also to get rid of the evidence of another of His most recent miracles—evidence that the kingdom of heaven was at hand. So they plotted to kill Lazarus as well, whom Jesus had just raised from the dead a few days earlier!

Now let's pull together the pieces of chapters 9 through 12 to arrive at the point I am desiring to make:

- Chapter 9: The scribes and Pharisees, being stuck in their traditions and personal ambitions, rejected Jesus as a *gift* from God, and rejected those who embraced Him.

- Chapter 10: Jesus declared that thieves, robbers, and hirelings care more about themselves than anyone else. They protect themselves and their own interests (*selfish ambition*), being unconcerned about the welfare of those in their care.

- Chapters 11 and 12: The religious leaders of the day plotted to kill Jesus, the man who demonstrated the kingdom of heaven, and Lazarus, one of many manifestations of the kingdom of heaven. Their intent was to silence that which was a threat to them because the people were turning away from them to follow Jesus.

So if Satan is not the real thief, who is?

THE REAL THIEF

The real "thief" in this story was the Pharisees, scribes, and other religious leaders of the day. By definition, a thief is one who robs by stealth rather than force. In other words, thieves act in ways that conceal their true motives and hope to obtain what they want without being exposed for who they really are. If then, the religious leaders were the real thieves, **how** and **what** did they "steal, kill, and destroy?"

How they did it...

The scribes and Pharisees used their laws and traditions to define what they would accept or reject. And while they looked "religious," they acted as thieves when they became more concerned about maintaining their positions of authority, prominence, and influence in their system of leadership rather than in *recognizing, raising up, and releasing* the manifestations of the kingdom of heaven in those under their care.

What they did...

The scribes, Pharisees, and religious leaders sought to steal, kill, and destroy two significant gifts from the people.

The first *gift* they wanted to take away was Jesus Himself. The people thrived on the hope Jesus brought to them as He manifested the kingdom of heaven in their midst. But it angered the religious leaders that the people would follow someone other than themselves. And since they did not receive who Jesus claimed to be, they plotted to have Jesus crucified to get Him out of their way.

The second *gift* they wanted to do away with were the *gifts* from heaven Jesus possessed and gave to the people—healing, deliverance, revelation, peace, and hope. The religious leaders could not provide any of those things and were jealous when the people chose to follow someone who did. From their perspective, they were losing ground; but that is always the way *jealousy* and *selfish ambition* views God-ordained change—as a threat. So they plotted to kill Lazarus too and eradicate any reminder of the *gifts* the people received through Jesus.

So if the religious leaders are "the thieves," where is Satan? Is he even in the story?

THE REAL WOLF

I believe Satan is the *wolf* mentioned in John 10:12. Jesus says, "He who is a hireling, and not a shepherd, who is not the owner of the sheep, sees the *wolf* coming, and leaves the sheep and flees, and *the wolf snatches them and scatters them."* When left unprotected by the real thieves (the religious leaders), the sheep gate is open for the *wolf* (Satan) to come and ravage the sheep. While a case could certainly be made that Satan has the capacity to "steal, kill, and destroy," his main objective in our lives is to bring deception and confusion (2 Corinthians 11:14) and devour what is ours when we don't walk with God (Malachi 3:11).

ARE YOU A THIEF, WOLF, OR *SERVANT IN AUTHORITY*?

You are probably wondering what this has to do with *servants in authority* and establishing atmospheres for receiving Spirit-led visions, directions, and strategies. Great question! Here's the answer:

All *servants in authority*, including both *visionaries and implementers*, are responsible to:

1. Steward the *gifts* (people) God sends their way,

2. Establish a positive atmosphere in which the *gifts* God gives each individual can be **recognized, raised up, and released** (manifested) to share with others,

3. Protect God's *gifts* (people) from harmful exposure to Satan (the wolf).

Just as God sent Jesus to redeem the world, God sends His children, some as *visionaries* and some as *implementers*, to accomplish their slice of His *strategic plan*. When *servants in authority* reject or fail to see and honor the *gifts* God has placed within all of His children; they *steal, kill, and destroy* the hope that lies within them to be both productive and valued. And when they fail to protect the sheep— even as *tenders*—they leave the spiritual doors wide open for Satan— the *wolf*—to come and deceive, devour, and destroy their lives.

The Amplified Bible version of Deuteronomy 8:18 says, "it is He (the Lord your God) Who gives you power to get wealth, that He may establish His covenant which He swore to your fathers, as it is this day." Within each person, God has placed *gifts* and abilities to convert time and resources into products and services that are of value to others (wealth). When *servants in authority* fail to **recognize, raise up, and release** the use of those gifts; they act as *hirelings*, not as *shepherds*. Interestingly, however, there is not only a negative impact on "the sheep," there is also a negative impact to themselves—the *servants in authority*. Whether a *visionary* or an *implementer*, they fall short of accomplishing the entire vision God has given them until they become able to move from being a *thief* to being a *true shepherd*.

Now, I must clarify one thing here before I finish out this chapter. I am NOT talking about resurrecting the *shepherding movement* that was prevalent in the 1970s and '80s. (This movement began as a mutual accountability group of four men, but as it gained widespread acceptance, there was a great deal of emphasis placed on obeying one's own "shepherd," which eventually resulted in controlling and abusive behavior in many circumstances.) In contrast to the controlling and abusive behavior that became the downfall of that movement, the kind of shepherding Jesus talks about in the Gospel of John is exactly the opposite. It's not about telling others how to live their lives and requiring their strict obedience to a shepherd's position of authority. It's about the dedicated shepherd laying down **his own** life for those around him. He is not focused on issuing commands, but on *protecting* and *raising up* the sheep to become all God intended and gifted them to be. As they do that, true shepherds fulfill their ultimate calling and reflect the heart of their Father in heaven.

Do you remember our discussion on the focus and role of a *tender* versus a *shepherd* in Chapter One? *Tenders* have a *tendency* to become *thieves*. True shepherds do not. Which one are you?

In closing, let's look at a verse I believe summarizes what I've talked about in this chapter. Though stated in the negative, it is actually very positive in that it contrasts the heart of the *thief* with that of the *Good Shepherd*.

Colossians 2:8

> See to it that no one takes you captive through philosophy and empty deception, according to the tradition of men, according to the elementary principles of the world, rather than according to Christ.

CHAPTER 13

Hiring, Firing, and Managing Others

The kingdom of heaven is like a landowner
who went out early in the morning to hire laborers
for his vineyard.
Matthew 20:1

I woke up early one morning with the topic of hiring, firing, and managing others on my mind. In times past, I would question why I was thinking about such things; but I have come to understand that such practical issues of living in this world are also on the heart of God. You might be wondering, "Why?" I believe it is because this subject, like every other chapter in this book, deeply and profoundly affects every one of His children— you, me, and everyone around us!

HIRING

"The kingdom of heaven is like a landowner who went out early in the morning to hire laborers for his vineyard...(Matthew 20:1)." I understand that the remainder of this parable as told by Jesus is not about hiring at all, but rather about the fact that regardless of when you come into the kingdom of heaven, we all receive the same benefit—spending eternity with God. But I believe there is something about hiring people that truly is part of the kingdom of heaven and on the heart of God. Let me explain by telling you about my experience with hiring.

While working at Boeing, I had the incredible privilege of being part of a team of managers that hired a wide variety of technical and professional men and women to work in manufacturing engineering (also known as production engineering). The difference between a "tech" and a "prof" was that *profs* possessed a Bachelor of Science degree in an engineering discipline from an ABET (Accreditation Board for Engineering and Technology) accredited college or university within the United States. The techs were everyone else hired to do essentially the same type of work—implementing tool and production plans to build parts and assemble the aircraft.

I truly enjoyed being involved in the hiring process. Quite honestly, it was one of those assignments I looked forward to and found fun to do; although it could also be mentally and physically exhausting at times! It was very stretching and challenging, and I always came away knowing deep inside that I had done a great service for the company and my peers. I also knew I was serving the people I interviewed, including the ones I had to say "no" to, by helping them get situated in the place where their God-given gifts and training could best be utilized for all involved. I never kept count, but considering the amount of time I spent reviewing resumes, representing the company at job fairs around the country, and participating in special hiring days, I wouldn't be surprised if I met with well over a thousand potential employees—even though hiring new employees was never my sole assignment.

As I am writing this even now, I am wondering why I enjoyed the hiring process so much. The only truthful answer I can give is that it felt very natural to me, like it was part of my gifting and who God made me to be. In hindsight, that now makes sense. I like to see people *raised up* into their potential and I have always been very comfortable asking people about themselves—where they are from, what they like to do for work and play, their dreams and aspirations, etc. In fact, I was that way even as a young boy.

I remember my dad enjoyed visiting different parts of the country, but due to limited finances, our family vacations typically involved camping. I grew up on the east coast of the United States; and by the time I was 13 years old, we had visited 40 out of 50 states, frequently staying in a state or national park. In addition, we were active in Boy Scouts—which included lots of camping and interaction with scout troops from all over the country and, at times, from different parts of the world.

In looking back on those days, I must have been developing and practicing the skills it takes to be skilled at hiring people without ever realizing that God wired me that way. As soon as we would finish setting up camp, I would wander around the campground, learning about the places other campers came from (their license plates were a dead giveaway!). And for some reason, I genuinely enjoyed listening to them talk.

I don't think I truly began to recognize the gift God had given me for hiring great people until another manager I worked with paid me one of the kindest compliments I had ever received. He told another one of our peers, "He hires great people." When I asked him what he meant, he shared how impressed he was with the ethics and quality of work he recognized in several of his employees that I had hired and that he would fight to keep them if someone tried to take them away. That comment made my day. Months later, he proved what he said when we were in our bi-annual salary and performance review meetings as a management team. He did everything he could to ensure those employees received significant salary increases and moved higher on the employee "retention rating" list.

The reason I picked those individuals was not the result of their education, or because they had an engineering degree, or had a long list of accomplishments that identified them as the "cream of the crop." The primary reason I hired them was because of what I saw in their hearts.

One of those individuals had no college degree but had an amazing understanding of what it took to serve others. In fact, she had been a food server for a number of years and wanted to make a career change. During my initial resume reviews, I had been intrigued by her resume. I could not pinpoint why, but I sensed she might have something the company needed—even though she had no direct experience working in an industrial manufacturing environment, let alone building commercial jet aircraft.

When she finally came in for her interview, it was very evident that she had an intrinsic quality for being able to recognize the importance of processes and order and had a gift for knowing how to put together a wide variety of seemingly unrelated pieces. She also had a sense of servanthood about her that made it easy for her to recognize what others needed. During my own years as a manufacturing planner, I knew that those qualities were gifts. You can teach almost anyone the technical aspects of production planning, but it is much more difficult to teach someone to have a servant's heart. Some naturally have it and some do not. And from my experience working with design and tool engineers, factory workers, and numerous other disciplines, one of the most valuable assets someone can have is being able to know what the customer needs; and the person with a servant's heart has the easiest time figuring out what that is.

Did I ever make a poor hiring choice? Yes, but only twice, that I recall. I hired both individuals primarily for three reasons: 1) their credentials, 2) the fact that they needed a job, and 3) our critical need for more people. In both cases, I had a slight "check" in my spirit, but I did not have any better selections available. I also wanted to give them a chance. The first individual was in his mid to late twenties. The other was in his early fifties.

The younger employee turned out to be an average performer who was more interested in becoming the leader of a political-social movement within the company than in doing what I hired him to do. The older one had an extensive list of accomplishments at a high executive level and told me he had lost his previous job in a major reorganization. But once inside, his methods for dealing with people and problems didn't match up to his credentials. Both of them worked for me initially, but then went to other groups, either the result of organizational reshuffling or their personal desires to try new assignments.

I learned a lot through both of those experiences. I was not soured on giving people a chance, but it did cause me to pay closer attention to what I was looking for in the people I was interviewing and what I sensed inside my own heart.

Some people talk about "getting the right people on the bus and getting them sitting in the right seats." I agree with that philosophy, but who are the "right people" and what is the "right seat"? Can you teach someone how to discover that, or is it more of an "art" or "gift"? Personally, I believe it's both an art and a gift. Those who are best at making great personnel selections are the ones who naturally look for the gifts and potential in others and desire to *raise them up* into all that God intends them to be.

Some of the other managers I worked with would focus primarily on college degrees and significant accomplishments. They tended to hire the "cream of the crop." However, it was very disturbing to me that the attrition rate for many of those individuals was typically 50% per year; meaning that within a year or so, 50% of those hired left our department to work in another department within our division or another division within the company. Their typical response when asked why they wanted to move on was, "I am bored." I honestly do not know the attrition rate for those I personally hired, but their names rarely came up in management reviews as having either left or recently expressed a desire to leave the department. In contrast, they seemed happy with their jobs and highly revered by their supervisors.

Why is it important to look for the potential in a prospective employee?

As I mentioned in an earlier chapter, regardless of our motivational gifting (what inspires us to get out of bed to go to work), we are called to serve, not to be served. This does not mean we are slaves, but Jesus said those that have a servant's heart are the greatest in the kingdom of heaven.

Therefore, when given the responsibility for hiring, utilize the privilege of being led by God's Spirit in the process. Get a vision of the qualifications required by the job and then ask God to highlight the applicants He wants interviewed. Interview with a servant's heart in mind and ask the Lord to give you interview questions and insight into the following as you meet with each prospective candidate:

1. Do they have the heart to serve the needs of others?

2. Can you recognize the *gifts* given them by their Father in heaven?

3. Are they a *visionary* or an *implementer*?

4. What are their personal and professional interests?

5. What potential do you see in them?

6. Do they have a teachable heart; a heart that is willing to learn whatever is necessary to *raise up* the *gifts* within them, even the ones they don't yet see?

7. Where are they on the *jealousy* and *selfish ambition* scale? Are they more inclined to "lay their life down" for the good of their co-workers and the group, or are they dedicated to making sure they win first at any cost?

8. Then finally, if you hired them to be under your care, are you prepared to *recognize,*

raise up, and release them into the destiny God has for them, even if that means you might only have them for a relatively short time?

If you stay connected to the Holy Spirit through the entire process, I believe you will not only obtain the right *gifts* (people) for your business or ministry, but you will be a *gift* to them in your role as an effective *servant in authority*, preparing and launching them into their destiny.

FIRING

I would like to tell you three stories about my personal experience with "getting fired," or at least the fear of having that experience. In all three instances, I learned a valuable lesson about being both an employee and a manager in the workplace. Fortunately, however, I have never had to go through that experience, and I hope I never will.

Experience #1

Before I worked for Boeing, I was a technical designer at the Synchrotron Radiation Research Laboratory (SSRL) that was part of Stanford University's Linear Accelerator Center in Menlo Park, California. Prior to that, I worked for a small family-owned company for seven years, so my move to the research laboratory was my first real job in a more professional atmosphere. At the lab, some of the most gifted physicists, engineers, scientists, and technical people from around the world were within a few feet of where I worked. I felt privileged to be there and the job was fascinating; but I also felt dwarfed in the midst of such academic and scientific mind power.

I was part of a small design team that consisted of a supervisor, a lead designer, and several senior designers. I was the low person on the totem pole, in both experience and technical capability. My drafting table was situated immediately behind that of my lead. We designed the equipment and support structures for experiments in which synchrotron radiation bombarded various types of materials and biological samples. The radiation changed the molecular structure of the materials it bombarded, resulting in significant discoveries for the medical and technology science communities. In fact, one day, one of the physicists showed us a piece of material he had just pulled out of his experiment chamber. It had a perfectly formed grid on the surface. When I asked about the significance of the result he replied, "This is the kind of pattern we need to make computer memory chips." I have no doubt his and other similar discoveries made their way to places like Intel, Hewlett-Packard and other high-tech manufacturers.

During my first week at SSRL, my lead gave me several drafting assignments to complete. As I completed each assignment, one-by-one I would hand them in for checking and then continue to work on the remaining assignments. My lead would then review my work, using a red pen to document his notes and circle any items that needed to be revised or corrected. One day, as I watched him "bleed" on my drawings, our supervisor kept calling him into his office and shutting the door. His office was right next to my drafting table and these meetings were happening at a very regular frequency, like every 15 minutes. After watching this process go on for over an hour (red markups, followed by a private meeting behind a closed door, followed by more drawing corrections) I began to break out in a cold sweat and feared the worst—being fired for inadequate performance. It made me so nervous that I finally got up enough courage to talk to my lead. I put down my pencil and triangle and made my way up to his table. When he gave me his undivided attention, I said, "If my work is not satisfactory or I'm not performing to your expectations, I will understand if you need to let me go." He looked at me somewhat surprised and with a smile on his face replied, "What do you mean?" I said, "All the red marks on my drawings, it looks like you slit your wrists. And you keep going into our boss' office, and when you return you keep making more corrections. If I'm not what you're looking for, I understand."

He started to laugh a little, which set my heart at ease. Then he said, "My visits to the boss' office and the comments I'm making on your drawings are unrelated. Every designer that comes to work here usually has had many other jobs, and every company has their own set of rules the designers need to follow. My red markups are to help you know how we want things done here." Then he said something that I knew was a gold nugget for me to put in my pocket. He said, *"The most important thing we look for here is a willingness to learn. If you are willing to learn, you will NEVER have a problem working here, even if you make a mistake."* Relieved and yet very humbled, I replied, "I want to learn everything you are willing to teach me."

I worked there for 18 months and then my wife and I moved to Seattle where I began working for Boeing. About a year later, I received a call from my former supervisor asking if I would come back to work at the laboratory. From his demeanor and request, I realized just how much they valued my contribution to their efforts. I also felt extremely privileged to have worked there and that my commitment to them and to learn whatever they would teach me had earned me a "good name" (Proverbs 22:1).

Lesson Learned
A genuine willingness to learn is like
gold in the eyes of your employer.

Experience #2

Before I accepted the job at Boeing, my dad and others told me of Boeing's reputation of going through significant cycles of massive hiring campaigns only to be followed by deep employment cuts several years later. However, after weighing the potential risks, I accepted the job and we moved to Seattle.

The day after new employee orientation, I showed up to my new work assignment ready to go but a bit nervous about what to expect. When I walked into the lobby of the building that would be my work home for the next 10 years or so, I and about 20 or 30 other new-hires met our escort, who gave us a quick tour of the building as we made our way to our assigned groups.

My escort introduced me to my senior lead, who in turn introduced me to my lead, whose initial response to my arrival was less than enthusiastic. "I told you before! I don't want no x#*%ing new hires!" After the senior lead shook his head in disappointment, I said to my new lead, "It's nice to meet you. I'm excited to be here and look forward to learning and working with you."

I knew my new lead's initial response had nothing to do with me personally. He was just reacting to the pressure everyone was under as the company was in the process of sending the more experienced employees from the existing airplane programs to help design, plan, and build two new airplanes that were due to rollout within the next couple of years...the 757 and 767. I was one of many new employees hired to take the place of those more experienced planners. And while such shuffling was regular, normal and necessary for the company to build new products, it was still hard on those given the responsibility to maintain the existing product lines and train the next generation of planners.

Sometime during that first week, I was going through the files in the desk to which I was assigned. The tab of one particular file caught my eye. It was highlighted and had large black letters that said, "**FIRING ORDER**." My initial reaction was, "Oh my God! They actually hand out a list of who they get rid of first just in case they have to let people go!?" Although very shocked, I avoided letting anyone know what I was thinking. I instead went to my lead and asked, "What's a 'firing order'?" After telling me it was a document that listed the sequence in which the airplanes moved through the production line, I snickered and told him of my initial reaction. He laughed and teased me for a while, but it was all in good fun.

I learned many months later that each organization within the company did have a "firing order" for employees in the case of an employment downturn. It was the "Retention Ranking" report, which was confidential and for management use only.

Lesson Learned
Do not let your imagination run wild!
Ask questions!!

Experience #3

I once served as a program manager of a major corporate strategic initiative for a new airplane program. I reported to a manager whom I both deeply respected and at the same time feared. I respected him because he clearly had a breadth and depth of understanding of the commercial aircraft industry that exceeded that of everyone else I personally knew. Not only had he come from within production engineering, which is where I had spent most of my career at that point, he had also travelled extensively for the company and was assigned to different company locations around the world that struggled to meet production quotas and time schedules. Consequently, he had a reputation as the "axe man" in some circles and had a very exacting and cold personality that made everyone in his midst fear for their career. He had a motto that has stuck with me for years, "I can't manage what I don't know," and yet telling him bad news was very intimidating because he was rarely kind in his response, often making the messenger feel like a failure.

At that time, the company was going through an upheaval of sorts in the form of a management culture change. For decades, the successful managers yelled during meetings at any hint of bad news. They also tended to ridicule and intimidate everyone they didn't know that came within their area of responsibility. My manager was raised in that environment for over 20 years and learned those tactics well. For those familiar with management theories, it was clearly a "Theory X" crowd.

The company, however, was getting a huge amount of pressure from the unions and other outside influences to revise their management culture to be more "Theory Y," which focused more on open communication, consensus, and "working together." That was a very hard transition for my manager because the "Theory Y" environment tended to result in indecision and whining, at least relative to the old "Theory X" methodology. Nevertheless, the company expected him to comply, and when the division managers received complaints from some of his subordinates (he managed a group of 120), he was sent to what was informally, and somewhat sarcastically, referred to by many as "charm school" to help him give up his "Theory X" ways in favor of a more "Theory Y" management style.

Following his return from "charm school," the documented employee satisfaction grade of his organization soared positively, which was a huge encouragement to him. However, when I attended a closed door meeting with a number of his other subordinates, the private report was nothing like that which was published; and it was only a matter of time before the truth came out. I remember leaving the meeting feeling very grieved for him because I knew he was taking huge steps to create a positive "working together" atmosphere in all his meetings and with those in his organization, but for some reason, the poison of the past was still being tasted and talked about by many.

For several days, I could not get his situation off my mind and I sensed God stirring my heart to talk with him about it. Unfortunately, the impression I also had was not much different than a servant of old seeking an audience with the king—if you approached the throne with bad news and had not been either summoned or had his favor, you could lose your head! I weighed my options and set in my heart to talk with him, but only if the opportunity arose.

Well, an opportunity arose! He called me into his office one afternoon to give him a status report on the project I was overseeing. As I finished my report, I became somewhat nervous inside. I was not sure I could actually say what I felt I needed to share, so I got up to leave. When I got to the door, I put my hand on the handle and started opening the door. Then I paused, looking at the floor and struggling with whether or not to tell him what was on my heart. He noticed I was pondering something and said, "Do you have something else to tell me?" "Yes," I responded, and then I closed the door and walked back over to the front of his desk.

I started, "What I'm about to tell you I know you could fire me for, but I'm willing to take that chance because I believe you have a right to know what's going on in your organization." For the next few minutes, I related to him what I had heard. When I finished, he asked what I thought he should do. That, in and of itself, was a shock! He had never asked me to give him personal advice during the entire two or three years I worked for him. After considering what to say, I answered, "Your employees don't understand what you are being asked to do. They do not understand the management techniques you were rooted in for over 20 years, and how you are being required to give those up and take on a completely different management style. You need to let your guard down and let them see that you are in many ways just like them, vulnerable and being required to change. They also need to know what you are actively doing to change. You need to ask them for their patience and understanding as you do whatever is being required of you."

He sat silent and did not immediately respond. I then said, "I will understand if you feel you need to let me go for what I've just told you." His only response was, "Thanks," and then he dismissed me, asking that I close the door on the way out.

A week or so after talking with my manager, the last of my subordinates (the group I managed was being gradually disbanded since our responsibilities were soon to end), asked to meet with me. He said he had just come out of a meeting with my manager and all of the non-management employees in his organization and could hardly believe what he had just heard. As he related what happened during the meeting, I realized my manager had taken my advice and the response of those who attended was extremely positive.

A month or two passed and my position as program manager ended. As I wrapped things up and prepared to assume my new assignment working on another airplane program, the time came for me to have a closeout performance review meeting with my manager. During that meeting, he asked me to assess my own ability for handling conflict in the workplace. I told him I felt I had a lot to learn in that arena, using as an example an issue of verbal abuse that had happened against me by another manager, one of my peers several months before. As I explained the details of what had happened he began to get very angry and seemed critical of me for not informing him of the incident when it occurred. When I told him that I did not want to be yelled at (he had done that a couple of years earlier), he clarified his reaction. He said he was not angry with me but that he would have had the other manager fired had he known about the incident, and that it should never have been allowed to go unreported. Had I heard him right? He just said that he would have defended me had I told him of the incident. I apologized for not telling him and realized I had just learned another valuable lesson.

Lesson Learned
When you lay your life down for others,
they will lay their life down for you.

All three lessons have been etched in my mind for many years and have become part of my foundation. To summarize, here they are again…

1. A genuine willingness to learn is like gold in the eyes of your employer.

2. Do not let your imagination run wild! Ask questions!!

3. When you lay your life for others, they will lay their life down for you.

The first two lessons were the result of my misperceptions about what was happening around me; somewhat frightening then, but funny now. The third lesson demonstrated a truth about the kingdom of heaven. In John 15:13 Jesus says, "Greater love has no one than this, that one lay down his life for his friends." When we become a true *servant in authority*, we will do as Jesus did—lay down our own life for the benefit of others; and in doing so, demonstrate the picture of God's love for the world.

MANAGING OTHERS

As I work with businesses and non-profit organizations, I frequently find two pieces missing in their operational processes that I believe are a primary reason for some of their struggles. The first piece is a **clearly written job description.** The second is a **performance management contract.** Let us take a brief look at both.

Job Descriptions

Have you ever been hired by a business or non-profit organization and shown up to work, only to find out that you have no idea what you are really supposed to spend your days doing? Or have you been hired with a basic understanding of why you're there but have no idea of the boundaries you are expected to work within? If you have, you know what I'm talking about. It's confusing from day one, and it doesn't ever really get any better.

Another scenario goes back to the *visionary* and *implementer* discussion we had in Chapter Four. *Visionaries* like to change directions—frequently. *Implementers*, on the other hand, need some degree of consistency to be effective.

Regardless of whether you are a *visionary* or *implementer*, you and the organization you manage or work for are most effective when EVERYONE has a clearly documented description of what is expected of them while "on the clock." This includes the person at the very top, the highest *servant in authority*, all the way down to the newest person at the very bottom of the organization chart.

Why is this important? Just as kids need structure in their schedule and home life to feel "safe," work environments are most effective when there is an appropriate amount of structure. Does that mean everything needs to be micro-managed? No, but it does mean that a lack of structure will most likely cause people to "fire-fight" issues rather than plan ahead and establish consistent processes that are effective in avoiding unnecessary surprises. ("Fire-fighting" is a term used to describe the tendency of some to wait for a crisis to occur before dealing with certain problems. Rather than making a plan and developing processes to minimize surprises, they actually thrive on their ability to "save the day.")

What if you are self-employed and work alone? Should you still have a job description for yourself? I would say yes, especially if you ever intend to expand and hire someone to take over some of your work. If you do not document what you do and what you expect to be done, how will you adequately *equip them* to effectively accomplish the work you are hiring them to do?

I recently coached a small business owner who allowed an independent contractor to work in her office and use her equipment to build her own business. Unfortunately, she had only a verbal agreement with this contractor and did not set up clear guidelines for her conduct. Problems arose when the owner instructed her assistant on how she wanted her client bookings documented, and the independent contractor convinced the assistant to do them another way. The owner's business problems grew as the independent contractor continued to "do her own thing." When the owner asked for help, I inquired about the existence of any written agreement between the owner and the contractor. There were no written agreements, and the lack of clearly documented boundaries and expectations forced a very confrontational showdown between the two, which eventually ended in them parting ways.

My point is simple. If you are a manager or employer, you need to provide a clear description of each employee's responsibilities. If you are an employee, you should request a written job description from your employer to avoid confusion as you endeavor to fulfill your responsibilities.

Performance Management

Probably one of the most valuable staff management tools I was introduced to a long time ago was *Performance Management*. Performance management was both a document format and a process used by managers and non-managers to define an employee's unique personal and business goals as they related to their specific job description. As a document, it specifically itemized an employee's responsibilities and expected performance goals as agreed to by both the employee and their manager. As a process, the document helped the employee keep track of whatever personal and business goals they were to accomplish during the next six to twelve months. The manager also used it during a bi-annual review of the employee's progress relative to the agreed-to goals.

Some balked at using the performance management tool, primarily because they saw it as another piece of paper to shuffle, another thing to do, and something that supposedly kept them from doing "real work." Unfortunately, some of the ones that had the hardest time with it were also the ones that were the least effective in their jobs. Personally, I found the process valuable in providing focus for myself and for those who worked for me.

What should be included in a performance management plan?

First, the elements of the job description must be included, along with measurable and specifically defined performance goals. Second, as a manager, I required my subordinates to include a section for their personal growth. This section could consist of personal development goals in an area that was not work related, and/or goals for developing their work-related skills because they wanted to progress in their career, or both.

Does the use of job descriptions and performance management reviews stifle flexibility and creativity?

I don't believe so. If anything, they do the opposite if used wisely. I found them to be a catalyst because they defined a baseline of performance that made it easier to see the personal and professional growth of each individual over time. At one point, I was overseeing 50 employees. As a manager, you cannot effectively help your employees reach their potential unless you know where they are beginning and can see their progress.

To state it more directly...

> If you, as a *servant in authority*, want to be an effective *shepherd* to those whom God has entrusted to you, to *recognize, raise up and release*, then the use of both a **job description** and **performance management review** will help you keep in close touch with those whom *you serve* and those who *serve with you.*

CHAPTER 14

Volunteers or Paid Staff?

The leech has two daughters, "Give," "Give."
Proverbs 30:15

I sat down to have a quiet time early one morning and asked God to speak to me about what was on His heart. I had no agenda for my quiet time and since it was the 30th day of the month, I opened my Bible and began to read Proverbs chapter 30. When I reached verse 15, I was unable to continue reading, so I asked God to explain that verse to me. This is what I heard Him say to my spirit...

*Leeches always **expect you to give to them** and their cause. And once you've given, they will continue to ask and expect you to give some more. They ask you to give of your time, your money, your possessions, your skills, and whatever other resources you have. They will even ask you to ask your friends to give. And when you stop giving, they move on to someone else. They do not really care about you personally or your situation. They do not really value you, and while they may value the gifts I have placed inside you, they will always* *want them without cost. They want you to help them accomplish **their vision** at **your cost.** Giving is a one-way street for the leech. But in My kingdom economy, giving is a two-way street, and My true servants in authority need to set an example in everything, including wages and payment for the services of My children.*

Over the past few years, I have been increasingly exposed to a philosophical ideology in a number of Christian ministries, churches, and businesses that causes my heart to grieve. It is the idea that it is more pleasing to God that they get people to volunteer to accomplish work that needs doing rather than paying people for their efforts. I used to wonder if there was something wrong with me, that maybe I had a bad attitude about volunteering. However, God has spoken so much to me about this that I am convinced it is not me but rather a revelation that this philosophy does not accurately reflect the true heart of God.

Now, just to set the record straight...

First, I am NOT saying there is anything wrong with having or asking volunteers to help with a project. There are times when we need to ask for volunteers, and volunteers need to respond (Exodus 36:2). There are also times when some will be inspired to volunteer out of the willingness of their hearts (Psalms 110:3).

Second, I'm NOT saying that everyone should be paid for every little thing they do.

And third, I am NOT speaking about those organizations that have set themselves as "100% volunteer organizations," where everyone from the top to the bottom is responsible for raising their own financial support to work with the ministry.

What I AM saying is that it is NOT God's heart that *visionaries* and other *servants in authority* EXPECT to always get free or cheap help to accomplish their vision. It is God's heart that ALL of His children are blessed and financially prosperous, and scripture does present a contrasting view toward the concept of volunteering.

I realize this may be a touchy subject for some, and I do not want to offend anyone, but while volunteers may be a great boon to those looking for help, it has a profoundly negative affect on a large number of God's other children when it is abused. As a result, I believe it needs to be reversed before the church will really be able to walk in the level of prosperity and corporate authority I hear discussed frequently. From what I see in scripture, the Bible talks more about money than any other specific subject, and more about fairly compensating workers and businesses than it does about God's children *volunteering* their time, skills, and resources to help a *visionary* accomplish his or her vision.

WHY IS THERE SUCH AN EMPHASIS ON VOLUNTEERING?

It is really about money. Sometimes the issue is that there is not any money, or there's not enough. Sometimes it is neither. Sometimes it is because the *servants in authority* either don't want to pay people for their efforts or they lack faith that God will supply the resources to bless everyone involved. It can also be the result of hidden agendas or because the *servants in authority* do not really value the gifts God has provided in the people He sent to help them "do the work of the ministry." Last, it can just be the selfish use of "it is more blessed to give than to receive."

I have literally had Christian ministry and business owners tell me, "I want to get everything for free," and "To be a good steward of what God has given me, I must always seek to get more for less." When I probed to understand the foundation of the belief system behind their response, they would essentially say, "God sees me as a better steward of His resources if I can get you to use *your resources* to accomplish *my vision*." I believe that attitude dishonors the children of God, both the believers and unbelievers, who have the gifts and skills they need to help them accomplish their vision. God's word is clear. He wants everyone to prosper, and *servants in authority* are not resonating with the heart of God when they expect to receive the services of those around them either without cost or at a subsistent wage while they themselves receive appropriate, and sometimes significant, incomes.

In 2 Corinthians 9: 7 Paul writes, "Each one must do just as he has purposed in his heart, not grudgingly or under compulsion, for God loves a cheerful giver."

If not kept in check, the I-want-everything-for-free mindset will tend to take advantage of the willingness of people to volunteer. How do they do that? By communicating, sometimes very subtly, that it is more "blessed," honorable, or spiritual to volunteer than to be paid. That may all sound good, but that mindset actually sets the stage for *servants in authority* to dishonor their brothers and sisters in the Lord; taking undue advantage of the very *gifts* God has sent to help them accomplish the work He has given them to do. How might that happen?

As you may recall, in Chapter 1 we talked about the difference between being a true *shepherd* and a *tender*. A *shepherd* protects the flock from predators at all times. A *tender*, on the other hand, just "babysits" the flock while on duty, making sure their immediate needs are tended to but not truly caring about the deeper and long-term needs of the sheep. If you are a *servant in authority*, protecting your flock as a *shepherd* includes ensuring that your staff and those that provide you with extensive help are not "devoured" by the financial pressures of everyday living. Protecting them includes paying them a livable wage and ensuring they have access to proper money management training, health benefits, etc.

Note that this is not so much an issue of how much money your business or ministry has in the checkbook. It is more a matter of where your heart is as a *servant in authority*.

Interestingly, the Lord spoke to that issue through the prophet Jeremiah in Jeremiah 22:13 and 17. Here is what the Lord said:

Woe to him...who uses his neighbor's services
without pay and does not give him his wages.
Your eyes and your heart are intent...on
practicing oppression and extortion.

Do other portions of scripture reflect that perspective? I
believe so. Consider the lives of both King David and King Solomon.

We will look first at David's situation at the end of 2 Samuel
24:18-25. David had sinned against God by taking a census of all the
Israelites, and God gave David instructions through the prophet Gad
to erect an altar to the Lord on the threshing floor of Araunah the
Jebusite. Aruanah wanted to give him the property out of respect for
David's position as king, but David would have nothing to do with
that. In verses 24 he says:

No, but **I will surely buy it from you for a
price,** for **I will not offer burnt offerings to the
LORD my God which cost me nothing.**" So
David bought the threshing floor and the oxen
for fifty shekels of silver.

Araunah was willing to give David all that he had to meet
David's need, but David refused to allow Araunah to foot the bill.
David insisted on paying for what he needed.

King Solomon did a similar thing when he became king.
Shortly after his father David died, Solomon set out to build the house
for the Lord that had been in David's heart to build. Now, Solomon
was not yet the richest King in all the earth, but his heart was to bless
everyone that worked to make his father's vision a reality. We will
pick up the story in 1 Kings 5:5. King Hiram of Tyre is reading the
letter Solomon had written to him.

Behold, I intend to build a house for the name
of the LORD my God, as the LORD spoke to
David my father, saying, "Your son, whom I
will set on your throne in your place, he will

build the house for My name." Now therefore, command that they cut for me cedars from Lebanon, and my servants will be with your servants; and **I will give you wages for your servants according to all that you say,** for you know that there is no one among us who knows how to cut timber like the Sidonians.

When Hiram heard the words of Solomon, he rejoiced greatly and said, "Blessed be the LORD today, who has given to David a wise son over this great people."

So Hiram sent word to Solomon, saying, "I have heard the message which you have sent me; I will do what you desire concerning the cedar and cypress timber. My servants will bring them down from Lebanon to the sea; and I will make them into rafts to go by sea to the place where you direct me, and I will have them broken up there, and you shall carry them away. Then you shall accomplish my desire by giving food to my household."

So Hiram gave Solomon as much as he desired of the cedar and cypress timber. Solomon then gave Hiram 20,000 kors of wheat as food for his household, and twenty kors of beaten oil; thus Solomon would give Hiram year by year.

The LORD gave wisdom to Solomon, just as He promised him; **and there was peace** between Hiram and Solomon, and the two of them made a covenant.

In return for Solomon's heart of generosity and desire to honor the gifts and skills of the Sidonians, God gave Solomon the wisdom he requested AND peace between his kingdom and the kingdom of

Tyre. Later on, in 1 Kings 7, Solomon hired Hiram from Tyre, a gifted worker in bronze (not the King), to make artistic additions to the temple using his metal working skills.

Moses wrote in Deuteronomy 8:18, "You shall remember the LORD your God, for it is He who is giving you power to make wealth that He may confirm His covenant which He swore to your fathers, as it is this day." Jesus said in Matthew 7:12, "Whatever you want others to do for you, do so for them." Then in Acts 20:35, the Apostle Luke references Jesus as having said, "It is more blessed to give than to receive." 1 Corinthians 9:14 states, "… the plowman ought to plow in hope, and the thresher to thresh in hope of sharing the crops." And the Apostle Paul tells Timothy in 1 Timothy 5:18 that "The laborer is worthy of his wages."

Servant in authority, **it is more honoring for you to actively seek ways to pay the people who use their gifts to help you than it is for you to expect them to donate their skills and time to serve you. By diligently seeking ways to pay them for their abilities, you are actually "confirming His covenant" with them.**

Does that preclude them from donating their time and other resources? No, but it puts the responsibility on YOU to give first.

God will honor your efforts to embrace His kingdom on this issue if you will wholeheartedly embrace the gifts He has provided you in the persons of His children. If you are a *servant in authority*, **he wants to bless his children** *through* **you**, but He needs your cooperation. It is an abomination for any *servant in authority* to proclaim the prosperity of the Lord, and then withhold that prosperity from those under their care—the very people they are to serve. If the Christian church is to be like a beacon on a hill, then we must be a positive example in all things, including how much people are paid.

I said earlier that it is not an issue of how much money your ministry or your business has in the bank. It is a matter of where your heart is as a *servant in authority*. If you truly desire to bless your staff and the others that help you with the wages they are worthy of receiving, then you will actively seek ways to obtain those resources. It will be very high on your priority list to increase their wages when the finances come in, and you will not be inclined to pay yourself first. But if that's not what is really in your heart, to make it so the staff whom you are called to oversee and serve don't have to struggle financially, then you will be inclined to use the increase of the team's efforts to build your own "paneled mansion" while your staff struggles to pay their bills.

GLASS CEILINGS

In industry and the church there continues to be, at least in part, a belief system that no one serving under a leader should make more money than the leader. To a degree, this has become less prevalent in industry as different career paths have been created. But I know of ministries where the financial glass ceiling philosophy still exists and is defended.

In the aircraft industry, there was a time when the salaries for all technical employees were limited, never exceeding that of the management, regardless of an employee's level or years of experience. At Boeing, that ended over 20 years ago during contract negotiations between the company and the union. The premise that facilitated the change was that great engineers and technical employees do not necessarily make great managers, and great managers are not always the best engineers or technical employees. However, because of the salary caps for non-managers, some "techs" and "profs" sought to become managers so their salary growth would at least keep pace with inflation. This created quite a dilemma for the company because there were far fewer management slots than non-management, and those employees that felt stifled due to the salary glass ceiling had to make a difficult choice—either stay with the company and watch their spending power deteriorate, or obtain reasonable salary growth by moving to another company or into management. Overall, upper management must have seen this was a "lose-lose" situation because they agreed to implement a career path with unlimited salary potential for employees that were committed to technical excellence and had no interest in joining management.

The church and other ministries would do well to adopt this philosophy. That fact that some have not chosen to become a senior pastor or other managerial path is irrelevant in today's society. It is the pride of man, that "Pharisaical spirit" that says, "If I'm in charge, you can't make more than me." If you are a *servant in authority* and that is the principle on which you base all salary determinations for those helping you, I challenge you to change your philosophy because you are not only hurting those you are called to serve, but you are hurting yourself. The fact is, every person on your staff is actually making you successful. If you do not believe that, then fire your staff and become a "one-man show," and see how far you get. You will undoubtedly have some level of success because God has given you gifts to help you make a living, but you will no longer enjoy the level of success and influence that only comes from the synergy created by the team that helps and supports you.

You might be wondering what this subject has to do with the focus of this book. The answer is—**everything**. Financial problems are one of the biggest reasons for employee dissatisfaction, business failure, divorce, and division in the Body of Christ. It is God's heart that we reflect and model His kingdom, and that we honor one another and the *gifts* He has placed within us. We **are** God's *gifts* to the world and to each other, and **we dishonor** the *gifts* (people) God has provided to help us **when we expect** them to freely give us their time, skills, and resources while we compensate them insufficiently to care for their own needs.

I will end with James 5:4 and Proverbs 3:27-28:

> Behold, the pay of the laborers who mowed your fields, and which has been withheld by you, cries out against you; and the outcry of those who did the harvesting has reached the ears of the Lord of Sabbath.

Do not withhold good from those to whom it is due, when it is in your power to do it. Do not say to your neighbor, "Go, and come back, and tomorrow I will give it," when you have it with you.

CHAPTER 15

From Glory to Glory, the Faithful Progress in God's Kingdom

But we all, with unveiled face,
beholding as in a mirror the glory of the Lord,
are being transformed into the same image
from glory to glory, just as from the Lord, the Spirit.
2 Corinthians 3:18

In 1998, I recorded the following prophetic word spoken over me during the three months I attended a class in Biblical counseling at YWAM. Some of what I documented was the word I received, but I also included my impressions as I listened. Here it is, quoted verbatim from my journal:

> Your future will not be the same as your past. You are in a rock quarry, moving and getting rid of the rocks in your life. Some are little and some are big. (The picture I got in my mind was that I was in a quarry surrounded by an infinite number of rocks of all different sizes.

My mind thought the quarry was very small, but as I got up off my hands and knees to expand my view, I was in a very large quarry, larger than I could take in with one sweep of my view.)

While you are moving rocks out of the way, God is also moving rocks for you, but He is using them to build new paths for you to walk on and follow, paths that will lead you to the place He has for you. (I also sensed He was hewing me out of the rock (Jesus), chiseling away to shape me so I would fit perfectly in the precise spot He has chosen for me on the wall of His spiritual house.)

Initially, I felt overwhelmed with the word I had received and was somewhat grieved by the thought that I had so many "rocks" to move out of my way. But I was encouraged by the fact that God was helping by moving some of the rocks for me. He wasn't just tossing them out of the way, He was converting the things that weighed me down to create paths upon which I would easily walk sometime in the future.

I share that to encourage you, that as a child of God, your future is not to be a repeat of your past, and that whatever you are going through today, God is in the process of turning your "quarry" into a beautiful garden path on which you will easily walk someday. That will undoubtedly mean different things to different people. For some, it will mean remaining in your current career, whether you are a professional, a manager, or a support to someone else, or even serving faithfully as a homemaker (which is one of the most difficult and important jobs around). For others, it may include a complete change of direction and venue. That certainly has been the case with me. Either way, you can rest assured of one thing—God will not let you remain as you are because He wants to see you become all that He intended you to be!

After receiving the prophetic word quoted above, I went home and looked up the word "stone" in my Bible concordance. I needed to see the picture I received in some positive context. What I found was 1 Peter 2:5-10.

> You also, as living stones, are being built up as a spiritual house for a holy priesthood, to offer up spiritual sacrifices acceptable to God through Jesus Christ.

> For this is contained in Scripture: "BEHOLD, I LAY IN ZION A CHOICE STONE, A PRECIOUS CORNER stone, AND HE WHO BELIEVES IN HIM WILL NOT BE DISAPPOINTED."

> This precious value, then, is for you who believe; but for those who disbelieve, "THE STONE WHICH THE BUILDERS REJECTED, THIS BECAME THE VERY CORNER stone," and, "A STONE OF STUMBLING AND A ROCK OF OFFENSE"; for they stumble because they are disobedient to the word, and to this doom they were also appointed.

But you are A CHOSEN RACE, A ROYAL PRIESTHOOD, A HOLY NATION, A PEOPLE FOR God's OWN POSSESSION, so that you may proclaim the excellencies of Him who has called you out of darkness into His marvelous light; for you once were NOT A PEOPLE, but now you are THE PEOPLE OF GOD; you had NOT RECEIVED MERCY, but now you have RECEIVED MERCY.

Here is what I get from that passage of scripture:

- As a "living stone," God is building me into a "spiritual house" so that I can take my place as a royal priest both in and of His kingdom.

- His purpose in making me a royal priest is so I can "offer up spiritual sacrifices acceptable to God through Jesus."

- His purpose in making me a spiritual house is so I can proclaim the things that are excellent about Him and His kingdom to those around me.

I would like to close this short chapter with a dream I had over 20 years ago. I did not receive the interpretation until a full two years later—long before I received the word about the quarry. Again, my purpose in sharing these is to encourage you that God IS changing you from glory to glory.

THE DREAM

My wife and I were sitting in the back row of a darkened church auditorium that was circular in design, kind of like a wagon wheel. The podium was elevated and was in the place where the wagon wheel hub would be. The aisles were like the spokes and the seats comprised the areas between the spokes.

A well-known preacher from Texas was the speaker, and there was only one spotlight shining on him. He spoke with confidence and authority as he walked up and down the aisles. My wife and I were sitting at the very back of one of the seating sections. I was seated on the corner and my wife in the seat next to me. As the preacher walked down the aisle where we were sitting, he stopped about 10 feet from my chair. The spotlight spilled over onto me. As I followed along in my Bible, He was facing the podium area and speaking enthusiastically. Suddenly, and out of context to his message, he turned and pointed directly at me and said, "And this man, dressed in a Levi suit, has a special call on his life." He then turned back toward the podium, resumed his message, and began walking back toward the podium.

I remember being stunned. I looked at the clothes I was wearing and thought, "I'm not dressed in a Levi suit. I am wearing a 3-piece powder blue wool suit."

I woke up in a cold sweat. The dream disturbed me because it was so vivid, and yet I had absolutely no idea what it meant. Two years later, my wife and I were attending a conference and one of the guest speakers said something that caused me to remember the dream; but this time I became painfully aware of what the dream was all about. The Lord said, "The dream was about you denying your call to serve as one of My priests. You thought the preacher meant you were wearing a suit made by Levi Strauss, but the suit he was referring to was of the Levitical priesthood. I have called you to be a priest in My house."

To this day, tears come to my eyes when I remember that dream–realizing the many years it was so hard for me to see what God saw in me. Yet in hindsight, I can see how God has been faithful to do what He speaks of in 1 Peter 2:5-10, which is quoted earlier in this chapter.

Some of you may not actually believe or even feel like a "royal priest" or a "spiritual house" at this time in your life. If that is you, I understand how you feel! You are probably in your own "quarry" and in the process of needing to move some of your own rocks out of the way. But please take heart; **God is working side by side with you to raise you up.** He is requiring you to move some of the rocks yourself, and yet He is moving some of them on your behalf. You are probably tossing the ones you can move as far out of sight as possible because you never want to see them again. He, however, is using the ones He is moving to create new paths for you to walk on. So be patient! The process of going from glory to glory takes time, and the ones that progress the farthest in the kingdom of God are the ones that are faithful!

CHAPTER 16

Now That You Know, Go!

*Go therefore and make disciples of all the nations,
baptizing them in the name of the Father and the Son
and the Holy Spirit, teaching them to observe all that I
commanded you; and lo, I am with you always, even
to the end of the age.*
Matthew 28:19-20

You have come to the last chapter and may be wondering, "How could I ever do all of that?" That is a great question, and I have a great answer for you! You can't; not without the grace, mercy, kindness and peace of God blanketing your spirit, soul, and body. Why? Because I believe everything I have shared with you in this book is God's heart for you, and gaining His heart is a process we walk through during our entire life here on this earth. It's called sanctification—the process of making us productive for spiritual use.

Some of what I have shared in the previous chapters may come quite naturally to you. However, the portions that are not as easy for you to see or walk in are the places where He wants to develop something deeper within you so that you can be an effective equipper of the next generation. Remember, His strategic plan is eternal, and we all have a part to play in fulfilling His purposes and plans.

I will be the first to admit that the things I have shared with you in this book are not necessarily easy to live out. Certainly, it has taken decades for some of them to develop within me. But the important thing to remember is that they do reflect the kingdom of heaven, and that is what we are called to make a place for on this earth.

When Jesus taught the disciples how to pray in Matthew 6:10 He instructed them to say, "Thy kingdom come, Thy will be done, on earth as it is in heaven." In Chapter 7, I talked about your *gift* making room for you in this world. I also talked about the fact that because we are **all** God's gifts to the world, our very presence makes room for Him in this world. Jesus confirmed this when He instructed the disciples to invite the kingdom of God to come and the will of God to be done on earth as it is in heaven. We **are His agents** to bring **His kingdom** to **this earth.** And whether we are a *visionary* or an *implementer*, as a *servant in authority* we have a primary role in *recognizing, raising up* and *releasing* His children to represent His kingdom with a pure heart and a pure mind so that NO ONE falls short of the grace of God.

So, let's summarize, by chapter, what we have covered.

Introduction: As a Christian, we have only one Leader—Jesus Christ; and we have only one Father—our Father in heaven. Many men and women of God aspire to positions of leadership; but God says we are to aspire to be servants of others—*servants with authority.*

Chapter 1: Jesus wants us to *shepherd* others. A true *shepherd* does not seek to rule or control others. A true shepherd lays down his own life to tend, guide, teach, mentor, and protect others.

Chapter 2: God has an eternal vision, mission, and strategic plan; and we all have a part to play in that plan.

Chapter 3: Our part in His strategic plan starts with seeking first His kingdom and His righteousness. That means focusing primarily on being in "right standing" with God, endeavoring to live in peace with those around us, and rejoicing in the fact that God is using our trials to develop within us perseverance, faith, and His character qualities.

Chapter 4: The world is full of *visionaries* and *implementers*, and we need each other.

Chapter 5: Children are a *gift* of the Lord. We never stop being children in God's eyes, therefore we are and always will be His *gift* to the world around us.

Chapter 6: God gives *gifts* to ALL His children; some come from the Father to enable us to survive, others come from the Spirit to help us hear and obey the Father, and finally the Son promotes those faithful to God and commissions them to equip the next generation.

Chapter 7: The *gifts* God has given us make room for us somewhere in the world. In addition, as God's *gift* to the world, our presence makes room for Him wherever we are.

Chapter 8: Every one of us has something to contribute in the midst of a gathering of people; regardless of our level of education, expertise, or responsibilities.

Chapter 9: Those who consider themselves "5-fold ministers" have one job—to equip people to do the work of the ministry. To equip means to **recognize, raise up, and release** people into their God-ordained destinies.

Chapter 10: To be effective, we must establish a "working together" atmosphere. That includes being willing to set aside our own success to ensure the success of others; forgiving; appreciating and extending kindness; serving others with an attitude of willingness to help them; and giving people a chance to grow.

Chapter 11: Ambition is good, but *selfish ambition* is demonic. Selfish ambition exposes itself through hypocrisy, self-promotion, and demanding honor; all of which are "stumbling blocks" for *servants with authority* to avoid.

Chapter 12:   People in authority who are afraid of losing their power or influence will steal from others whatever threatens their power. They are the "thieves" Jesus warns us about.

Chapter 13:   Regardless of our position in an organization or family, God is our ultimate master and we will answer to Him for how we served as both a worker and *servant in authority*. How we go about hiring and managing people is extremely important to God because we represent His heart to all of His children. He has given them as *gifts* to help us and entrusted us to help them become effective *servants in authority* in their own right.

Chapter 14:   God loves a cheerful giver, and the most generous givers should be the *visionaries* and *servants in authority*, not the volunteers. As *servants in authority*, we should be willing and seeking ways to pay people generously for their time; especially when their God-given gifts cause us to prosper.

Chapter 15:   God is making each of **one** us into a spiritual house and a royal priest, able to proclaim His excellence skillfully and effectively to others.

Jesus says in Matthew 28:19-20, "Go therefore and make disciples of all the nations, baptizing them in the name of the Father and the Son and the Holy Spirit, teaching them to observe all that I commanded you; and lo, I am with you always, even to the end of the age."

He has promoted you from a leader to a *servant in authority*— authority to serve others, not to require they serve you. Your promotion is part of His plan for your success because He has *recognized* the *gift* you are and the *gifts* He has placed within you; He has been and will continue to *raise you up* and prepare you for your future; and He has seen fit to *release* you into this new stage of life. As long as you remain one of His trusted *servants in authority*, He will continually entrust to your care some of the people *(gifts)* He has given this world. And just as He has done with you, your assignment in serving them is to:

1. *Recognize* the gifts He has placed within them,

2. *Raise them up* in the gifts He has given them, and then

3. *Release* them to take their manifestation of His kingdom into all the world.

Now that you know, go!

About the Author

Michael Adams is an accomplished manufacturing and business implementation professional with over three decades of experience spanning technical design, commercial aircraft manufacturing planning, program and project management, strategic planning, and business process design.

Prior to founding *MSA Strategic Solutions* in 1998 to provide strategic planning services to small businesses and non-profit organizations, Michael worked with The Boeing Company in Seattle, Washington and the Synchrotron Radiation Laboratory of Stanford University in Menlo Park, CA, and Kenco Engineering of Roseville, CA.

Michael and his wife, Debbie, currently minister the heart of God together through *Heart of Heaven Ministries*; providing inner healing prayer counseling to individuals and couples, *"Choosing the Heart of Heaven"* workshops, and discipleship groups. For more information, you can visit their web site at www.heartofheavenministries.com.

If you are interested in having Michael speak at your church, business, retreat, or conference, please send your request and contact information to info@heartofheavenministries.com.

www.ingramcontent.com/pod-product-compliance
Lightning Source LLC
LaVergne TN
LVHW011233080426
835509LV00005B/483